UNLEASH
D↑FFERENT

Achieving Business Success
Through *Disability*

RICH DONOVAN

Published by ECW Press
665 Gerrard Street East
Toronto, ON M4M 1Y2
416-694-3348 / info@ecwpress.com

Cover design: David A. Gee
Author photo: © Dale May

LIBRARY AND ARCHIVES CANADA
CATALOGUING IN PUBLICATION

Donovan, Rich, 1975–, author
Unleash different : achieving business success
through disability / Rich Donovan.

Issued in print and electronic formats.
ISBN 978-1-77041-448-8 (hardcover).
ALSO ISSUED AS: 978-1-77305-268-7 (EPUB).
978-1-77305-269-4 (PDF)

1. Success in business. 2. People with
disabilities--Employment. 3. Labor market.
4. Marketing. 5. Consumers. I. Title.

HF5386.D66 2018   650.1
C2018-902586-7   C2018-902587-5

The publication of *Unleash Different* has been generously supported by the Canada Council for the
Arts, which last year invested $153 million to bring the arts to Canadians throughout the country,
and by the Government of Canada. *Nous remercions le Conseil des arts du Canada de son soutien.*
L'an dernier, le Conseil a investi 153 millions de dollars pour mettre de l'art dans la vie des Canadiennes
et des Canadiens de tout le pays. Ce livre est financé en partie par le gouvernement du Canada. We also
acknowledge the support of the Ontario Arts Council (OAC), an agency of the Government of
Ontario, which last year funded 1,737 individual artists and 1,095 organizations in 223 communities
across Ontario for a total of $52.1 million, and the contribution of the Government of Ontario
through the Ontario Book Publishing Tax Credit and the Ontario Media Development Corporation.

ONTARIO ARTS COUNCIL
CONSEIL DES ARTS DE L'ONTARIO
an Ontario government agency
un organisme du gouvernement de l'Ontario

Canada Council   Conseil des Arts
for the Arts   du Canada

Canada

PRINTED AND BOUND IN CANADA   PRINTING: FRIESENS   5 4 3 2 1

MIX
Paper from
responsible sources
FSC
www.fsc.org   FSC® C016245

To the hundreds of millions of people with disabilities around the world: this is a story of one man owning his identity and acting on that identity. It is my aspiration that you rise as powerful consumers to embrace your identity and demand better experiences. To the global institutions seeking to attract people with disabilities as customers and employees: start by listening directly to your customer, and then act on what you hear. Do these things, and you've changed the world forever.

JUST THE BEGINNING

I had prepared for this moment for weeks, months, years. In some ways, I had been preparing all my life. Yet somehow it hadn't quite hit home that it was really going to happen—at first, probably because it was so far off, and then because it was just so colossal. But now it was here. I was at the New York Stock Exchange (NYSE), about to ring the opening bell before three hundred million observers. Back when I was a trader, that bell had marked my starting line each day. On this day, it would mark the start of trading of a new stock market index—one that I had created. The Return on Disability Index would be the world's first to recognize disability as a driver of shareholder value. It would measure the performance of companies that provided products, services, and careers to people with disabilities. By ringing the bell, I was about to launch 1.3 billion people into the global economy. No pressure.

Even in that busy room, my thoughts went back to a night in the bar with my crew at Columbia Business School, when I first voiced my ideas. "You know, guys, I'm getting all these requests and calls from disability groups, and I did the math. This market looks big. Nobody's really looking at it." My friend Dustin looked at me and said, "You know, Rich, you're a successful guy. You've done well, and there's this big body of people out there who need leadership. Isn't it kind of incumbent on you to step up? I mean, this is something that you can do. This is something that you're uniquely qualified to do."

Most people don't get to see the client lobby of the NYSE. It's a gorgeous room, full of artifacts: ancient ticker tapes, memorabilia, and screens playing videos featuring the operations of listed companies. Anyone who steps inside will quickly understand, if they didn't already, that this is not just a place where billions of dollars are exchanged each day. It is a place with history and meaning.

The NYSE staff greeted our party that had been invited for the opening bell ceremonies and led us to a room where they gave us name badges and a medallion to mark the day. We were then ushered into a boardroom that seemed to come straight out of a movie set. An impossibly long table extended into the distance. At the end was a kind of altar where you could imagine the leaders of the Stock Exchange in, say, 1894, discussing the fates of companies and building the institution that today is the world's biggest arbiter of capital.

We had a brief reception to celebrate the occasion. The NYSE set a strict cap on attendees, so we only invited our biggest supporters—those who had been instrumental in getting our concept off the ground and who embodied what we were trying to do. We had the head of the UN agency on disability. My Luu, the former global innovation, solutions, and policy director at IBM, was there. We had representatives from Pepsi; Mark Wafer, a disability champion formerly at Tim Hortons; and many others.

Our partners at Barclays asked me to give a speech. This was bound to be interesting, because most of the people in the room—NYSE officials, Barclays colleagues, other business people—had never heard me speak before. I think the Barclays team especially expected a rah-rah speech on building community—the typical charitable approach. At that point, ours was a boardroom relationship. They didn't know my speaking style and had no clue what I was going to say.

I was genuinely overwhelmed by my surroundings and the idea of launching this new financial instrument that would recognize people with disabilities as a market. I ended up giving probably the hardest-core business speech of my life. I don't generally write speeches—I speak from the head and the hip. Toward the end, I remember saying, "This is not the end of the journey, this is just the beginning. This is where we focus on the economic potential of 1.3 billion people in the world who have disabilities. We put the power of financial capital behind these lives of phenomenal potential. That's what this institution was created to do, and now we're going to do it with disability." I ended the speech with a call to action: "We've got some work to do, folks. Let's get to work." I don't usually speak that way—I generally default to facts and the logic that flows from those facts. But in that moment, something compelled me to make that call to action. In the moment, it dawned on me that we were about to trade disability as a market for the first time. I owed it to the thousands of people with disabilities whom I had met to unleash my own passion. I owned my own identity as a person with a disability.

It was time to head to the trading floor. As is typical for me when I'm in an older building, I took the back way, the way the public never gets to see—which I kind of enjoy. I walked past offices and conference rooms and closed doors, and I could imagine some of the world's great inventors walking through those halls. Once again, it dawned on me that we were breaking new ground by leveraging a centuries-old institution in a new way. I smiled and thought, *Okay, let's go.*

To reach the podium on the balcony, we had to go up a flight of stairs. Some folks were obviously concerned about me getting up those stairs. Cerebral palsy (CP) gives my walk a distinct wobble, so if you don't know me, you might think that climbing stairs was a problem. The NYSE had assigned me a security detail of three big guys. If I had had a wheelchair, they probably would have carried it. The attention was wholly unwarranted, but I found it grounded in genuine concern. Working with me requires people to think differently, and many certainly were.

I waved the big guys off and walked up the stairs just fine. When we got to the landing, I sat down and got my briefing: "This is what's going to happen. In ten minutes we're all going to go up on the podium, and at 9:29:50 you're going to ring the bell. You press the button and hold it for exactly ten seconds. Then . . ."

"Wait a second," I interrupted. "There's a button?" At that point, my mind felt like it was about to explode. I had spent the early part of my career working on automating equity trading at Merrill Lynch, and I assumed that the opening bell rang thanks to an algorithm automatically linked to a clock. Nope.

"Are you sure you want the guy with CP ringing the bell?" I asked jokingly. Part of my disability functionally impacts my fine motor control. In other words, I shake a bit. *Great*, I was thinking, *I'm going to be the guy who double-rings the Bell.* Given the respect I have for the institution of the New York Stock Exchange, I didn't exactly relish that prospect.

One of my Barclays colleagues said, in a stage whisper, "Isn't that kind of the point of what we're doing?"

Yes, we were putting people with disabilities in control. What blew me away, however, was that in this day and age, at the New York Stock Exchange of all places, where everything today is about computers, where financial modeling software conducts trades automatically and petabytes of data fly along fiber-optic superhighways every nanosecond of every day, you needed to put your finger on a *button* to ring a bell announcing that trading was open for the day. The enormity of the moment came down to the simple pushing of a button. It was perfect.

When our group moved up to the podium, we had an amazing view. There it was, spread out before us: the trading floor of the New York Stock Exchange. I looked out over the packed room, a room I had first gaped at, bug-eyed, as an undergrad from Canada's York University. A room that I'd surveyed with calculating eyes as an MBA candidate at Columbia Business School. And a room through which I had put billions of dollars during my time as a trader at Merrill Lynch. To say I was nervous would be a colossal understatement. For the next nine minutes and fifty seconds, I was utterly focused on that button. It was all I could think of until 9:29:50 finally came around, and I placed my left index finger on that button and pressed down using every newton of force that I could muster. The bell rang. It was loud. I had every muscle in my body trained on that fingertip. You could have come at me with the entire defensive line of the New York Jets and I wouldn't have budged. After precisely ten seconds, I released.

For me, the game shifted at that point. Up until that moment, the lives of people with disabilities did not include one of the primary inputs of everybody else's lives, which is financial capital. Now we had a platform to build from. A lot of people would look at me ringing that bell and see it as a crowning achievement, but I looked at it as a beginning, as a way to start something new. I looked at all of the things that needed to happen from that moment forward to bring this market into alignment with every other market of its size. It was mind-boggling. Change is not simple. You can't brush it across the canvas like paint to make it magically appear. You can't give a speech to a billion people and expect change to occur. It's cumulative. First people make slight changes in what they do in their daily lives, both within institutions and in their interactions with those institutions. Multiply that by the number of institutions that we have, whether companies, brands, or governments, and it quickly adds up to billions and billions of new actions. To me that's both very daunting and incredibly exciting.

Until we change the way we think and act with disability in every way, we are wasting the potential and futures of hundreds of millions of people. That's why I must ask that as you go ahead and read this book, you, also, change the way you think about disability. So don't expect that I'm going to offer you stories about my struggles to overcome limitations to do the everyday things that other people take for granted. A, boring. B, I learned from a pretty early age that if you want to have success as a person with disabilities, you focus on knocking the ball out of the park every chance you get. Because guess what? We will be judged on our results whether we have a disability or not. So as you read my story, please don't handicap my performance, if you'll excuse the expression, by feeling sorry for me. And please don't come to me looking for inspiration. This book is intended to be 100 percent free of inspiration porn. I'm a business guy with a market-based vision for a new way to build economic value by attracting and delighting people via the process of thinking differently. It happens to have been informed by my personal experience of CP and my observations of people with disabilities acting in consumer and labor markets. I've written this book to share what it takes to make this vision come true—a vision that will "unleash different." I invite you to join me on the journey.

ONE

GROWING UP
DIFFERENT

CHAPTER ONE
THE SHORT BUS

I grew up in the bedroom community of Newmarket, outside Toronto, in a modest beige split-level home with a small front- and backyard and a driveway. When I was five, in 1980, my day started earlier than any other kid's on the block. I took the long ride to kindergarten. That's just the way it was. Rain or shine, slush or snow, at 7 a.m. my mom and I watched for the short yellow bus to come around the corner and pull in front of our house. Then I pushed my walker down the driveway and boarded for the hour-and-a-half bus ride to Toronto.

The bus disgorged us at the Ontario Crippled Children's Centre (OCCC), an antiquated name for an institution that was progressive in its time because it worked hard to treat each child as an individual who could reach his or her full potential. Twenty-two women had founded the school in 1899 for children with chronic illness and disability. In the 1980s it was renamed the

Hugh MacMillan Centre, and as of 2017 the center is Canada's largest children's rehabilitation hospital focused on improving the lives of kids with disabilities.

Until I left that school, after third grade, I knew I had a different life than the other kids in my neighborhood. No one else rode a bus for ninety minutes twice a day. That sucks up a lot of time. We did typical school activities—painting, jumping around with gym equipment, learning to read—the only difference being that every child had a disability. I grew up thinking that disability was pretty normal. My younger brother, Mike, didn't understand disability until he was five or six. He tells the story about one of our neighbors telling him that we couldn't go somewhere because I was crippled. Mike was devastated at the time. To me it was no big deal. Mike remembers having that conversation with my mom, and of course she told him, "Well, you know, he kind of is."

As a kid with cerebral palsy, I would engage in "therapeutic" experiences like swimming and horseback riding. The thing that sticks with me is not those activities themselves, but the car rides back and forth with my dad. They were full of conversations about what business success looked like. Dad talked to me about how you drive quality, what process is. I had a good grasp of the precepts of Six Sigma before my tenth birthday.

Dad was technically trained in civil engineering and had a degree in economics and finance. He worked over thirty years for AMP Inc./Tyco Electronics, a global industrial company that made electrical/electronic interconnection systems. He acted in a variety of capacities, marketing, sales, product management, product development and engineering, and at the end of his career was the Americas region operations manager for the energy division. The way that he thought, focusing in on process and quality, influenced me tremendously. It formed the foundation of how I became so efficient at doing things so that I could keep up with everyone else. His process-oriented way of looking at things was incredibly powerful for me; it still informs everything I do.

Now that I look back on it, I can see that Dad was working with me so that I would learn how to engage with my world as a participant. Never passive, never a victim. Dad fostered learning wherever he could. He put benchmarks in front of me and said, "Go do this." I think he knew that the world I lived in would be very different from his world. Instead of low hurdles to jump over, he set goals for me that were wholly unrelated to disability. If you ask him about it now, he would say that he just got out of my way, but that's Canadian humility talking. He pushed me. He didn't do it by kicking my ass. He did it in such a way that it broadened my horizons. I'm doing the same thing with my son. I point out things that are beyond his current concept of reality—to stretch him and push him. It's good parenting for any child—with a disability or not. I never remember Dad saying, "You can't do that." He didn't treat me any differently than he treated my younger brother, Mike. In those days, no one would have expected someone with cerebral palsy to eventually make it to the trading desk of one of the world's greatest investment banks—except Dad, Mom, and Mike.

That's one key to how I was raised. My parents helped me see my life as composed of bridges to cross, not barriers to keep me away.

Parents of children with disabilities approach me all the time wanting to know what to do with their kid. "Do what you do with any other kid," I tell them. I think that's the mistake that most parents make. They think they must adapt and change—I don't buy that. Of course, every child is different, and parents ultimately will decide what's best for their kid. That said, never let your child be limited by your own perceptions of their disability.

CHAPTER TWO
BLOWING UP BARRIERS

During the 1970s and 1980s, it wasn't easy for kids with disabilities or their parents. If you were disabled or had friends or classmates with disabilities during those years, you know what I mean. Kids with "special needs" seemed to have a spotlight shining on them—for better or worse. As policy changed to "allow" kids with disabilities into school, many were watching to see what would happen—parents, teachers, and lawmakers. Policy is a piece of paper. I and millions of other kids were managing the day-to-day realities of the successes and failures that accompany change.

As someone with a disability, I had no obvious role models to follow. I didn't know any people with disabilities I could look up to; there was nobody to say, "He did that, she did that, you can do that." I owe a big thank you to my parents and to many other kids' parents who threw dynamite at the granite walls that existed in the educational system. That's what changed institutions to include people like me.

Mom and Dad talked to us a lot about what people think and say versus what they do. And it's true. What comes out of your mouth rarely matches what your hands produce. I suppose that Dad recognized some basic level of intelligence in me and thought to himself, *Hey, if that kid's going to succeed in life, he's going to need to harness that intelligence.* Knowing how his brain works, he was preparing me for that: simple life lessons to prepare me for what I thought was going to be an engineering career.

If Dad is the rational, process-oriented influence in my life, Mom is the one who gave me my feistiness and appetite for risk. She's an extraordinarily passionate woman who likes to live a little bit on the edge. She wanted to push everything all the time but in a very Canadian way. Mom is very polite, very nice. She was a teacher by trade; her role was keeping things on track. From her own upbringing, she has a profound sense of family. Mom was one of thirteen brothers and sisters from Chicoutimi, a town in northern Quebec. I remember visiting her family in this town surrounded by the Canadian boreal forest and the Saguenay and Chicoutimi Rivers that flowed to the St. Lawrence. We had good times relishing Quebec's culture and enjoying family and friends in a setting unique in North America.

At eighteen, Mom had left for California to work as an au pair. She was the only one in her family to leave Quebec. Imagine what that would have been like: doing what no one else had done in her family, traveling all the way across the continent alone, with just a few words of English. Mom always had a real hunger for discovery. She probably said to herself, *Well, I can stay here and join the family motel business, become somebody's wife, and that's it for the rest of my life, or I can set my own path.*

The Donovan household was always technologically advanced. We were one of the few families in our area that had a computer in our house in . . . I think it was 1981. In fact, we didn't have one computer, we had three. Dad had access to all this technology because his company was starting to build computer components. At age seven I was playing *Football Manager* on my brand-new TRS-80, an early microcomputer first sold by RadioShack in 1977. For writing, I used an electric typewriter with a key guard. You would put your finger in a hole to hit each key. I typed everything, because I couldn't write. Okay, technically I can write, but good luck reading my scrawls. I got into video games before most people knew what they were, but I was also into sports, especially hockey.

Ours was a big hockey town; Newmarket had every level of hockey below the NHL until the Saints left. Mike, who is eighteen months younger than me, grew up playing minor-league hockey and baseball. I loved going to his games. He was a pretty good minor hockey player and freakishly tall for a Donovan. We are not known for our physical stature. My grandmother was four foot eleven. Mom is just over five feet. My dad is probably five foot seven. Somehow Mike ended up being over six feet tall.

I had no access to organized hockey because it wasn't available for people with disabilities at that time, but I got my fix on the driveway and on the street. I couldn't run without crashing, so I always played goalie. I'll never forget getting goalie pads for Christmas when I was eight years old. I slept in them for days.

I was, and still am, a Toronto Maple Leafs fan. When I was a kid, my church was Maple Leaf Gardens, the historic arena in downtown Toronto. You would come into the Gardens and be surrounded by sixteen thousand people, and I was in awe. Those games are my favorite memories. I did the same thing there as at my brother's games: I yelled and screamed at the refs and at the other team. I always enjoyed coming to Toronto to see them and getting wowed by the buzz of the city. Streetcars and the CN Tower, huge buildings . . . I've always been a city guy. I was small enough that my dad would carry me. It would have been a disaster to walk the streets of Toronto with my walker. Because I never really walked. I ran everywhere. In fact, I modified my walker to get places quicker. Most walkers have two posts and two wheels. I had my dad put four wheels on it. It didn't have any brakes, and I went through shoes like race cars go through tires.

Mike and I were both rambunctious, physical kids. We bonded fast in early childhood and spent our formative years messing around outdoors. The Donovans love sports and competition. Dad played football at the Montreal Institute of Technology—he used to kid us that he went to MIT—where he was a punter and a kick returner. "Not in the same play, obviously" was our running joke.

Part of being physical was taking risks. Not stupid risks, but all the same I probably spent half my childhood with one injury or another, which just about drove my mother up a wall. By eighth grade, I had acquired an electric scooter so I could "walk" further and faster. At my wedding Mike told the story of us riding it—how he would jump on the back and I would let go of the brakes and take off down a hill. One day we did it on a curve, took it too fast, and rolled it. I never broke anything, but I pulled muscles, sprained ankles, and strained shoulders playing sports and messing about.

One of the things we loved to do more than almost anything else as a family was boating. I pretty much grew up on a boat, first sailboats and then powerboats when my mother got tired of waiting to get where we were going. Dad and Mom figured out early on that sailing was something we could do as a family because people with mobility issues can function well in the small space of a sailboat. Mike and I picked up sailing easily. Dad entrusted me at an early age to run the boat safely. A few hours north of Toronto, Georgian Bay, which contains a Canadian national park, offers thousands of islands and narrow channels for cruising but also contains lots and lots of rocks. When handling a sailboat, you needed to focus 100 percent. For me, it was a hell of a lot easier and a lot more fun than walking.

When my parents first decided to buy a boat, they also bought an inflatable dinghy with an outboard motor. Mike and I had a blast taking turns driving and bombing around the water. One day we were jumping waves and the air above us exploded as a Royal Canadian Air Force CF-18 Hornet fighter jet flew about five hundred feet above our heads. We went wild, waving at the pilot as s/he made a few high g-force turns directly above us. To exit, the pilot decided to go vertical right above our dinghy. I thought the roar would split the sky.

My family liked to go sailing for a week at a time among the Thirty Thousand Islands of Georgian Bay. We'd sail up the east coast of the bay, up past Parry Sound. We had a few close calls, but one crossing of the North Channel was particularly hair-raising.

We were due to have our chartered sailboat back at the marina the next day, but a storm was brewing. The other couple with us were experienced sailors, so my dad and his friend decided to go for it and make the return trip. If we'd had better information, we probably would not have made that decision, but as sailors will tell you, anything you live through makes you a better sailor. We had thirty-foot waves and sixty-knot winds coming at us. The kind of weather where you put the storm jib out and suddenly you're doing six knots. It was scary. On the Great Lakes you get short wave intervals a few seconds apart. No sooner do you hit the bottom of a trough than you're immediately going back up in something like thirty-foot chop.

Mike and I thoroughly enjoyed it, laughing at Mom, who was anchored in the gangway, terrified. But Mike also made sure I was stable, ensuring my butt stayed planted in the cockpit while the boat was heaving up and down. When we arrived at the marina, ambulances were there for some racing sloop sailors who had sustained broken bones and concussions getting thrown around their boats by the pounding waves. "I'll never forget that day," Dad has said more than a few times.

Why am I telling you all of this? Because I want you to understand that I had a wonderful and, in so many ways, very normal childhood.

My parents wanted me to have every opportunity to be successful at whatever I wanted to do, and that occasionally meant pushing me in certain directions. The first big push came in third grade. It was 1982, and the province of Ontario had passed a new law offering mainstream integration, making it easier for kids with disabilities to be educated in the public schools along with everybody else.

Not only was Canada the first country in the world to protect persons with disabilities in its laws, Ontario became the first *province* to add these provisions to its laws.

The Human Rights Code was amended to protect against discrimination "because of handicap." The law said that "handicap" meant "real or perceived physical, mental retardation or impairment, mental disability or a disorder." Today, the law says that people cannot be discriminated against because of "disability." Notice the quotes. This was accepted language from the most forward-thinking government globally in the 1970s. The language makes me cringe now, and that cringe is a tiny sign of accomplished change.

My parents faced a big decision: was I going to continue with the ninety-minute ride from Newmarket to Toronto every day or go to a local school? The question came up partly thanks to Mrs. Post, a tough German woman who taught me at Sunny View Public School (attached to the OCCC). She was a character. If you screwed up, you had to memorize a poem and recite it for the class. I was a bit of a wild child in that school—I thought I owned the place—so I memorized a lot of poetry.

Mrs. Post never minced words, and she didn't mince them

when she told my parents what to do. "Get him out of here," she said. "He doesn't belong here." They took her advice and set about having me start fourth grade in the mainstream environment of St. Paul Elementary School in Newmarket.

When they first contacted the principal about transferring me there, the principal put up a fuss. "Oh, he wouldn't be ready," he said. "That's too much, too soon." But my parents went down to the local school offices for a meeting, and when they returned home it was all set. While one might assume this was an enormous change for me, that is not how I remember it. I was eight years old. It was a new school, not a new world. That is the reality of change.

CHAPTER THREE
HOCKEY HELMETS AND TENNIS BALLS

I am not someone who wants to dwell on the past. In fact, I tend to discount it, simply because of the concept of sunk cost. If it's done, it's over. You can't recover something that's already spent, so there is no point in worrying about it. We remember so that we can learn, but any concern or regret is wasted. There is no point sitting there wishing you could reverse that thing that happened. You're never going to recover sunk costs. The next ten seconds matter. The last ten seconds don't. That's the way the world is. For me it's always been a case of considering the future to figure out what the most important ten seconds are—and building a path to get there, to that moment, where I will be at my best.

Preparing for those ten seconds can take decades. One meeting I had in 2016 with the Canadian minister of justice had been seeded twenty years earlier. You never know where things are going to come from.

During my jam-packed work periods, my wife, Jenn, some-times asks, "Do you have to take this meeting now, when you have so much going on?"

"Yes, because you never know," I tell her. You never know what contact or thought provocation will lead to the next break-through. A large part of success is being at the right place at the right time. Your odds of finding successful paths increase if you put yourself in more places at more times. In each situation, I try to declutter and focus on what I need to get done to get to those ten seconds. The rest is just noise.

A dream doesn't become a reality if it stays a dream. You've got to do things to make it happen. You can't will your way to success.

In hindsight, the shift to a mainstream school was a bold step, the first big step toward those ten seconds. I was one of the first kids in Ontario with a visible disability to go to a main-stream school. It was obvious that I was different because I came to school with a walker that had tennis balls as feet and wore a hockey helmet, ostensibly to protect me in case of falls. Of course, I never fell and hit my head, but that's how things were done back then—there was no concept of dignity. It was all about getting it done, about finding and minimizing the risk. At eight years old, I didn't question what I was given. I finally got rid of the helmet and the walker in sixth grade.

I enjoyed the first three years at St. Paul's. I have fond memo-ries of just doing my thing, probably because in the earlier grades, children are harmless. I'm not saying I was an angel—in fact, I was a bit of a troublemaker. Not only in school, but at home too. I would rewind a John Cougar Mellencamp song with the word "shit" in it and play that part repeatedly, piping it throughout the house. I wasn't exactly a rebel, but I ran away from home once when I was seven or eight because I wasn't allowed to do some-thing I wanted to do—I don't remember what it was. I packed a bag and told Mom and Dad that I was running away. I got all the way down the block with my walker. Then I came back. Dad asked what happened and I told him it was too far. He had trained me well—my analytical abilities were working just fine.

◾

The first instance of bullying that I remember was in seventh or eighth grade. I came home and told my parents what these kids were calling me. A bit of advice. If you wish to keep my respect, don't use the word "retard" around me. While I don't believe in censorship or "wagging a disapproving finger"—people are free to be complete barbarians and act irrationally—I do believe what you do and what you say have consequences. Words and actions reflect who you are.

"Rich," my mom said, "you're going to have deal with that kind of thing the rest of your life. You are going to run into people like that. So how are you going to handle it?" They figured I could cope, and they were right.

A kid with CP is an obvious mark. I was lucky because back in fourth grade a few of the girls had taken me under their wing. Classmates Lisa, Stacey, and Danielle were my bodyguards, or my advocates, and that helped a lot. But the taunting bothered me, especially in my early teens. I became sensitive to it. Puberty is hard. Becoming an adult physically and emotionally can be a painful journey for all of us. We become aware of how we are different, of how others see us, and how we believe we do or don't "fit in." With a physical disability, this transformation can be even more self-conscious. Initially, I didn't understand what the teasing meant. I had not experienced it before. It was just jerks taking shots at me, and that was tough. But then I had to begin to grapple with what that looked like and felt like, and how I would own it as an individual.

Probably everyone with a disability deals with this when they go to school, but it was especially difficult at that time. Since I was one of the only kids at my school with a visible disability, I was a target. Back then, people didn't teach kids about accepting other people who were different. In fact, some parents didn't like having me around.

The bullying probably had more to do with jealousy than anything. I did well academically, and the guys taking the shots were not exactly the sharpest tools in the shed. I tended to deal with it quietly and just ignore it. I rarely talked back. I wouldn't really find my self-confidence until high school, around the tenth grade.

The high point of my elementary school career was winning the science fair in eighth grade. I won with a project on airfoils, otherwise known as wings. Dad and I built a wind tunnel out of plastic and a working wing out of cardboard, drinking straws, and plastic wrap. It was powered with a bedside fan. The tunnel had slots, so you could change the angle of the wing by moving the struts up and down to make it fly and land. It was very simple but very robust. That was an early learning of success. I walked into the gym after the judging, and everyone was looking at me. I was just beginning to wonder why, when I saw the blue ribbon on my entry. I promptly fell on my ass—I think I did it on purpose.

CHAPTER FOUR

BAD TO THE BONE (FOR A GEEK)

I n ninth grade I moved to Sacred Heart, a big high school in a residential neighborhood in Newmarket. My family had just moved to Aurora, an adjacent town to the south. That was another adjustment. We chose Sacred Heart because it was the only school in town with an elevator. It was crowded, and I would probably have been eaten alive simply walking down the hall if I hadn't just gotten my first scooter. All of a sudden, I went from being at a disadvantage on everyone else's terms to being on my own terms. Overnight, I was the fastest. I was the biggest. People got out of *my* way. I didn't realize it at the time, but it began to change the way I moved through life and even the way I thought. Up to that point I was always introverted—I wouldn't say shy, exactly, but hardly extroverted. The scooter played a role in changing that.

I entered an accelerated learning program, something called PACE. It was a different peer set—we were all geeks (a badge

I still wear proudly)—and we were pushed to think beyond the norm. The PACE Learning System lit the fire, opening my world to a more content-rich universe full of science and math, physics and engineering concepts. These were the things that I was most drawn to at that point. In my studies, I had been actively preparing for a career as an engineer, but that was before I discovered economics. I really like complexity. I like moving parts. The more complex a thing is, the more I want to do it. For me, economics is not a closed system where you know all the flows, all the variables. Economics deals with human beings, so there are literally billions of variables. I find that fascinating, and this was why finance would later become my major at York University.

◗

Most great business leaders understand branding very well. It's the sizzle that entices people to look at the steak. I have always valued steak over sizzle—I do sizzle reluctantly. But I know there is value in it, and over the years I have learned to be a little bit more P.T. Barnum. Last night I was out to dinner with Jenn. We walked into the restaurant and somebody said, "Didn't I see you on TV last night?" So there is something to the sizzle. Great ideas don't have much impact if nobody knows about them.

My first encounter with sizzle was in tenth grade. I took theater, not entirely by design. Taking an arts course was mandatory in high school, but with my fine motor skills, I wasn't about to take a painting or drawing course. So, I took the theater course. I fell in love with it. Soon, I was acting, writing, producing, and trying to put on shows. I'm still in love with theater because it enables us the chance to build a world of possibility and then bring it to fruition.

My friends staged a surprise production for my sixteenth birthday. I was at my friend Rob Fortin's house—he and I were going to go out for dinner and some comedy, or at least that's what we had planned. Other than us, as far as I knew, the house was empty. Suddenly Rob said, "What was that? I thought I heard something. What the hell was that?" We crept downstairs. Two guys in black ski masks appeared. One of them took out a gun and shot Rob. I jumped about a mile high. There was blood everywhere. I was freaked, screaming, "Rob, are you okay?" Then ten or twenty people came out and shouted, "Surprise!"

The inside joke was that I hated sudden loud noises. With CP, sudden loud noises make you jump, hence their choice of a starter pistol. The school production we were involved in at the time required a gunshot, and we had to figure out how the character I was playing could be offstage when that happened, because for sure I would jump. There was no avoiding it.

Rob Fortin, Ron Cadieux, Kristen Blanchard—they were my closest friends in high school, "the crew." Kristen and I never officially dated, but we had a sort of platonic romance. She was probably my best friend throughout high school. We talked a lot and were always over at each other's houses. She was smart, attractive, politically savvy, liked to take risks, and loved going places. We went to Toronto to go to concerts, the theater, museums, restaurants, and comedy clubs. Sometimes I would take her to school dances, but sometimes I would take other girls. It wasn't a standard relationship. We encouraged each other along our chosen paths. It was a mutual admiration society that lasted for about five years, and though I don't know where Kristen is these days, I am still so grateful for our incredible friendship.

◀

Tenth grade was a big year. Not only did I join the theater club, I also indulged my growing enthusiasm for politics by gaining a seat on student council. I became one of the school's public relations officers, doing the marketing for school events like dances and writing a weekly article in the local paper on behalf of the school. Sometimes I had fun making controversy. I remember a Valentine's Day article that was very tongue-in-cheek. "This is supposed to be a world of equality," I wrote. "So why just flowers for the girls? Where are my flowers?" An early foray into non-traditional markets.

By the time I hit eleventh grade, I felt ready to make a run for school president. My platform was World Youth Day. I wanted to invite global heads of state to Toronto for a conference about what global youth could do for society. That went precisely nowhere with the Ministry of Education, but the kids loved it and so did the media. I remember having a couple of calls with Colin Vaughan from City-TV to see how we could make it work.

From watching Reagan, Bush, and Clinton act and speak, I started to develop my own style—well, in my mind, at least. I had to learn how to give a speech and do it in a way that people would know what the hell I was saying. I had not only content challenges but also delivery challenges. With my CP comes the gift of "slurred" speech. That's where process came in. Because I was a slow typer, I never wrote drafts. Everything I wrote was a final version. It was the same with mathematics. I got through high school and university level calculus without writing down a single formula. When I wrote an article or a speech, I drafted it in my head, correcting and revising until I had it where I wanted it. Only then did I commit it to paper.

Running for school president meant I had to learn how to shake hands, how to greet people . . . and how to shrug off rejection when it came my way. One day during that campaign, I came home in tears because I found out that the president of the PTA had said there was no way that her school would be led by a person with disabilities. I was crushed. Here was an adult in a position of authority, slamming me for my disability.

My father sat me down at the kitchen table and gave me some tough love. He said, "Look, Rich. If you want to be on top, you had better get used to people trying to knock you off. Because that's what happens when you change people's realities. You've got two choices: you either develop a thicker skin and let this stuff bounce off you, or you can live in misery."

I grappled with that for a couple of days and then took my dad's advice and made it my own. I decided, hey, heck with 'em if they can't take a joke. I began to take the stance "It's your problem if you can't deal with disability. I'm coming. You can either come with me or get run over." That was one big turning point in my life. I went from reacting to what happened around me to being in the driver's seat. In fact, I learned to love messing with people. I learned to enjoy making people think, *What? Wha . . . what???* when dealing with their own perceptions of my disability. It was their problem, not mine. I guess this is when I started realizing I was going to unleash different.

At that point in my life, I wanted nothing to do with disability, and I wanted to run as far away from it as I could. That wasn't entirely mature, but I was a high school student. At that time, I decided the way to go about life was to be as good at everything as I could be. To be the best. Second-best wasn't good enough.

My campaign slogan was "Bad to the Bone" simply because I had a bumper sticker on the back of my scooter that said it. In fact, it was the opposite of what I was. I was no tough guy, but I did have an advantage over other candidates because I had somehow managed to co-opt the entire cheerleading squad into acting as my display team. I remember sitting with the squad in one member's basement a day before the campaign, plotting strategy. Twelve cheerleaders and I plotting political strategy. You can't make that up. At that age, I already understood what constituted steak and what constituted sizzle. I just wanted the steak but somehow managed to get the sizzle too.

My friends Kristen, Randy, and Andrew were my biggest help with the campaign, mostly sticking up posters and giving me moral support. Of course, it wasn't a massive, orchestrated effort like it is with mainstream politics. It was more like, "Hey, do you want to help out?" We slapped up a couple of posters, gave a few speeches. I didn't have a crack political team behind my campaign. I built a coalition of as many folks as I could cobble together. I was in with many kinds of crowds at school. Not deep in but kind of dabbling in all of them. Looking back, I can see that it's the way I have always done things. I put the ideas up front and let them sell themselves. The machine will take care of itself. Some people do the exact opposite: they build a machine to sell fluff. Consumers have a long history of figuring out where the value is in the marketplace, whatever the spin is.

During the two-week campaign, candidates got up in assembly and spoke three times over the course of a day. Once for the ninth and tenth grades, then the eleventh and twelfth, then finally the thirteenth. We had to speak again in front of the whole school in a different assembly just before the election. I had this big razzmatazz production number planned with all the cheerleaders. But then the administration decided to nix it because they didn't think it was becoming of the office. It didn't matter. I won anyhow.

Becoming school president was an early public success. It showed what was possible in life. Talking to people, coming up with innovative ideas, building relationships—that's what this was about, and I was good at it. As president, I made some relationships that lasted. It got me closer to some friends I already had, and I made new ones as well. Through the York Region Presidents' Council, I met Noble Chummar, the president of St. Elizabeth in Thornhill. School presidents met once a month to see if there was a common goal we could work on at the regional or provincial level. Noble later went on to the London School of Economics to study law and is now partner at Cassels Brock, a corporate law firm in Canada. He also was an adviser to Prime Minister Chrétien. We kept in touch, and he now advises me on business issues.

I think that part of the reason why I decided to run for president—and won—was that at that time, I approached life as if I didn't have a disability. To me it just wasn't there. It was somebody else's construct. My life was just my life. Ignoring my disability was my way of dealing with it. My philosophy was to just go at it, take a bite. I don't ever recall feeling that it was a problem. But there were exceptions, notably in my relationships with girls. I never had a girlfriend before grad school. Not that I wasn't interested—I always remember having an interest in someone. But trying to make it work wasn't a priority. I always found something more important to do—and let's face it, I was avoiding the issue. It was a difficult prospect. When you have a disability, dealing with sexuality takes a great level of maturity. It also takes imagination. For young people, having a date, a relationship, sex: these steps all required confidence and a certain way of carrying yourself. But these experiences also required a little bit of a script, whether from the movies or stories from friends. How many movies, TV shows, or books do you encounter involving people with disabilities falling in love? For an adolescent, it was like walking a mental tightrope without a net.

I had zero self-confidence when it came to women until I was twenty-nine or thirty years old. It just didn't exist. Part of that was just being a kid from Newmarket and not being worldly. I didn't really get it until I had my career on track. Before that I had to deal with all kinds of other things, like getting into the best schools and learning what I needed in order to get where I wanted to go. It wasn't like I had a playbook mapped out and placed "girlfriend" after "career," but school and career were always my priorities because they allowed me to focus on doing the things I needed to do to become successful. Knowing what I know now, I would have had so much more fun.

A lot of people with disabilities never figure it out. These are some profound human nature issues that most people stumble through, including me. I had been looking at the dating thing from a very emotional perspective. It's just who I am. I'm a guy who likes Disney, I like a happy story, I liked the idea of walking off into the sunset. I had always seen love as this magical thing where everything should be perfect, with an eighteen-piece orchestra in the background with angels and harps.

When you have a disability, the odds are not stacked in your favor in terms of dating. If a "typical" guy meets a hundred women, he might have a chance to build a relationship with ten of them. A guy like me would have to meet a hundred women before having one legitimate conversation. Human beings are wired to default to ingrained perception. That's biology and brain science at work, also called heuristics. The perception of disability is so strong and negative in most brains, it can be challenging to trigger attraction. Making a connection can take longer. And that doesn't guarantee attraction. A lot of people with disabilities (PWD) give up before they begin. They figure that it's just too hard. They go on dates and spend an hour with someone before they realize that this someone is afraid of, or turned off by, or just can't deal with disability. A lot of people can't cope with the rejection. I know for a long time I couldn't. It is painful and lonely and frustrating. But it's something PWD can deal with and *can* figure out. I hadn't figured out romance in high school, but I had learned how to build relationships with people—including the cheerleading crew—and those social skills would serve me later.

CHAPTER FIVE

WALL STREET CALLS, UNIVERSITY BEGINS

I switched my career goal from engineering to finance in eleventh or twelfth grade. There were two triggers, the first of which was chemistry. When I got a 72 in chem, I decided that maybe I had better make a change. I had never gotten a 72 in my life. Two things were going on: I didn't have an aptitude for chemistry, and trying to structure molecules in my head was too difficult. If I'd had Excel at the time, I could have done it. I can work out a two-dimensional formula without putting pen to paper; trying to structure a three-dimensional formula in my head was too hard.

The other trigger was the movie *Wall Street*. I saw it in 1990, three years after it came out, and I was enthralled. I had become convinced that the market approach was the ultimate mechanism for allocating resources. In market theory, everything could be solved with the two crossing lines of supply and demand.

Everything. I was just blown away by it. When Mike and I first watched *Wall Street* in our basement rec room, I thought, *Wait a second, there's a job I can do that gets me close to market theory? Cool!*

"I'm going to New York!" I crowed to Mike. I pointed at the screen. "I'm going to do that." There was no doubt in my mind. That was my path.

Mike, as he recently told me, was like, *Oh yeah, you're going to New York, that's great,* not figuratively rolling his eyes as brothers should.

Naturally, to get to Wall Street, I wanted to go to Columbia University. It was an A-list Ivy League school, it had a strong economics department, and most of all it was in New York City—close enough to Wall Street to access the network. The thing was, I needed a scholarship, and unfortunately not even my high school grade point average of 98 percent was good enough for a full ride as a foreign student at Columbia or any of the other Ivy League schools I applied to. At age sixteen, I wasn't savvy enough to tell them that I had CP. I was oblivious to the implications of making this part of my story to the wider world. At that stage, I was still determined to prove to myself that CP wasn't going to hinder me from success. It never entered my head to disclose my disability.

Staying closer to home, I decided to attend the business school at York University in Toronto—an excellent school best known for teaching accounting and finance at the time. Founded only in 1959, York is now the third-largest university in Canada, a major research and higher education facility. The campus sprawls over a sizable chunk of uptown Toronto. Well regarded in Canada, York now routinely ranks high in global tables. Dad earned his economics degree at York at night school after he graduated from the Montreal Institute of Technology. Mom attended teacher's college there, also in night school. Anyone who puts themselves through night school after a full workday has my respect—I saw how hard Mom and Dad worked to better themselves alongside working to pay the bills. Some folks think I come from a wealthy background, but my parents worked their asses off.

Back when I applied to Canadian universities, the way you did it was by checking a box on a form. It was all about GPA. This was the third year that the York bachelor of business administration had been in existence, and something like four thousand people applied for 135 slots.

I entered York determined to get to New York City and work on Wall Street after I graduated. My preoccupation with the market theory roared into an intellectual fire after my first economics class. Professor Ridpath was a market conservative at a university where some professors were still giving credibility to the socialist merits of Stalinist Russia. He and I got along very well. He grounded me in the basics of market economics and taught me how supply and demand worked. I still use those simple concepts in my work every day. I'm a big believer in simplicity amongst complexity, in bringing things down to their base levels.

Ridpath taught the curve-driven economics pioneered by economists such as John Kenneth Galbraith. According to Galbraith, economic behavior is rooted in the simple premise that markets always clear. The phrase refers to equilibrium, when supply and demand achieve balance and therefore the perfect price.

Consider the price of an iPhone. During the first year of Apple's brilliantly staged release of a new phone, demand wildly outpaces supply, and customers will pay the highest price for the phone itself (setting aside the economics of buying discounts through new phone plans and so forth). Three years down the road, that same model iPhone will be offered by major retail outlets for something like $400 cheaper as demand dwindles to a fraction of its first-year frenzy. Somewhere between the release date and year four, you'll find a market clearing inflection point where Apple's profit is reasonable and so is the price, in the eyes of most consumers. That's when the price stops falling.

This aspect of economics may seem like magic. It's not, of course. It's in the data, but you must wade in. You must understand what drives demand, where supply comes from, what the cost structures are, and what the market is likely to pay for any given thing.

Developing that knowledge can take a lifetime. Understanding market forces is especially important for me because I'm applying them to change disability. Everything I'm doing with Return on Disability goes back to that simple statement: markets always clear. Always. It's just a question of how long it takes.

I couldn't get enough of this stuff in university, but in other ways, my first two years at York were a struggle. I was doing academic work in an environment where I had to change the way I previously did everything. Since I couldn't write, I would take a quantitative test, like a calculus test, and because I couldn't write they would give me a proctor who would write for me. Proctors are volunteers, and most of them tended to be people in the softer sciences.

Once, I was taking a statistics final and one of the questions involved averages, including writing out formulas. I dictated a simple formula to my proctor, which was "Mu = sigma $(x, y, \ldots n)/n$." The proctor heard what I said but had no exposure to math and ended up scribing "meow = stigma ex-why end over end." After I had laughed myself silly for about twenty minutes, I realized the basic communication problem. To show what I knew, I had to come at it in an unusual way. I was trying to fit in with academia's way of doing things and it was degrading my performance. Where I used to be an A-plus student, now I was a B student. In class, I was always one of the top reports. In projects, I would get As. Tests were another story, and it was extremely frustrating.

In second-year calculus, I realized that I had to change something. I was getting Bs and Cs on tests. It wasn't just the proctors' fault. I was being tested on the assumption that I had been taking notes in class just like everyone else. In coming up with answers in calculus, the convention is to build up an arsenal of written proofs before getting to the final formula. Most people see this derivation as a process of steps. I see it as one big line. I didn't write out proofs. I learned concepts natively and constructed this stuff in my head. I didn't have to recall formulas, or why it was x or why it was z, because I simply knew how to apply the concepts. Later, when I got to Wall Street and was using derivatives and other applications that required pure mathematics, I didn't have to refer to a template. I knew the stuff. I could have conversations on a level that my peers just couldn't because I didn't have to use formulas as a rule. I had a true understanding of the concepts and the mechanisms behind them.

But at this moment, my advantage in application turned out to be a real hindrance on tests. I simply hadn't taught myself the formulas that everyone else had written so many times they were on automatic recall. I knew that when you get out of school nobody cares about the proof, but I had to get through school first. I started thinking about dropping out. I had never been held back, and I had never used disability as a reason for not competing at the highest level. I didn't want to be judged by a different set of rules. I was still denying my disability. I was failing because I just wasn't dealing with it.

Finally, I asked myself what the heck I was doing. This is the first memory I have of moving to active adaptation when I encountered a gap in a system that undervalued PWD. I needed to fix it or fall further behind. I no longer could avoid it. I needed to find a solution. I didn't know what the solution was, but that was where the dean of students at the business school came in. I approached her and explained what I was dealing with.

"That's easy to fix," she said. "I'll talk to your profs, and you can do your tests directly with them." She went to my profs and said, "Hey, has this guy been performing in your class?"

They all said yes but noted that I performed terribly on tests. And that's all it took to fix things. I found a way to convince these guys that I knew what I was talking about and went from a B average to an A average overnight.

At that time, York didn't put much focus on getting a summer job, which I thought was strange, so I was on my own. Between my second and third year, I sent out 117 résumés to banks, insurance companies . . . any company that had anything to do with investments or corporate treasury. Cold calls. I got a few interviews: Air Canada, Bombardier, Royal Bank, TD, and Citibank.

At Citi, an HR executive named Janice Bowman interviewed me. Years later, I remember asking her what went through her mind that day when we first sat down together. "After the interview," she said, "I marched up to the hiring manager and said exactly this: 'You must give me a good reason not to hire this guy. He's that good.'" She also said that it was a big step for Citi because they were not in the practice of hiring people with disabilities. That was 1995.

Robin Plumb ended up being my first boss at Citi. He was great. Robin taught me the foundations of the language of risk, which informs everything I do now. I see risk as a language, much like mathematics. In the investment world, everything comes back to risk. If you understand the different forms of risk and their nuances, how those components affect your portfolio's risk profile, you'll understand investment better than anyone else.

I like to say that when you're trained in risk, you will always be a defensive driver. Analyzing risk is about understanding the probabilities of good and bad outcomes without fear and making a judgment. In driving, the value of arriving at your destination five minutes sooner does not outweigh the risk and cost of an accident. In finance, the challenge is to understand what the data is telling you about the "right" gains and the "right" losses to expect. The same is true of games of probability such as poker or blackjack. It comes down to "Know when to hold 'em, when to fold 'em."

On my second day at work, I was going down to get lunch when I struck up a conversation with the other guy in the elevator. He asked if I was new to Citi and I told him that I had just started the day before. He asked what I did, and I told him that I was a summer intern on the risk-management team, specifically looking at the derivatives portfolio. He said, "Welcome to the team. I think you'll really like it here. It's a wonderful place to work." That was Rick Lint, then-CEO of Citi Canada. He was right. I liked it a lot.

Working at Citi showed me what a large global company was like. I got exposure to the New York and London offices, and the diverse ways that capital flowed. I got to work on big deals. The first deal I saw was the failure of Olympia & York, a large real estate development company. O&Y was one of the largest bankruptcies in the history of the world at that time, and Citi was one of its largest creditors. It was an incredible introduction to global finance. I had never been in a business meeting before in my life, and here I was in meetings with the heads of divisions, working out risk profiles on different deals, in different currencies, in different investment vehicles. I loved it.

That summer, I got up at 5:30 every morning to take the GO Train—a commuter train funded by the government of Ontario— from Aurora to be in downtown Toronto for 8:00. I guess they liked me, because they asked me to continue working during the school year, which of course I accepted, structuring my classes so that Fridays were free. I had the job everyone on my career track wanted: working at a U.S. bank. It was rare for a Canadian kid to get one. If you could get in, you could get transferred down to the U.S. in a few years. At that time, if you were Canadian and you wanted to be at the pinnacle of finance, you wanted to be on Wall Street.

At York I was surrounded by folks who were like me—ambitious, ready to blow the doors off the program. We started a study group and became great friends. While writing this book, I reached out to my best friend, Fernando Pica, to tell me what he remembered. Here's what he wrote in an email.

> I remember seeing this skinny guy drive in to class on his scooter. He was hard to understand and often quiet. Nevertheless, I recall thinking to myself there must be something to that guy. You don't just get into this program on sympathy. We became friends in statistics class. Rich was in charge of designing our operating models. We discovered there that his mind worked differently than ours and he could process more variables than most of us. That gave us a working advantage over other teams.
>
> We loved to work in Rich's dorm room. It was notorious for being poorly stocked of food. The only thing to eat was ginger snaps because they were easy for him to eat and they could be purchased in the cafeteria on his meal plan. Rich's dorm room was also a good source for loose change. Given he had little use for it, we often collected it. It was handy on pub nights. [Since my hands tend to be shaky, carrying loose change presented an unnecessary challenge. In those days I dumped change in a desk drawer. Now it goes in my son's piggy bank.]
>
> We had to work hard. It was a tough program. We gave Rich no slack, and he barked back hard when he thought we were letting him off

easy. On one occasion, we had a presentation to make for a portion of our grade. We were worried that Rich's speech would be difficult to understand and hurt our mark. We deliberated it and decided, "Who cares, everyone will need to be quiet and pay attention." We got an A.

In my third year at York, I got my first taste of New York. My friend Marty and I took a couple of Mexican exchange students, Ricardo and Guillermo, down for a road trip. New York was where it was at—the pinnacle of success. Marty drove us all down to a cheap hotel out by LaGuardia Airport in his powder-blue K-car, and then we hit Manhattan. I remember getting closer and closer—the skyline, the apartment buildings, the endless city lights combined in my mind to create a floating spectacle like an advanced civilization you see in a sci-fi movie. Then, as we entered the city, it was walls and walls of enormous height. If I sound like a kid from a little suburban town in Canada called Newmarket, well that is exactly who I was. It was simply awe-inspiring, the kind of thing where your head is on a swivel and you're just looking up and around, taking it all in. Everywhere I looked there was something just blowing my mind.

We did the Twin Towers, the Statue of Liberty, the usual tourist things, but we kept our wits about us. New York was a rough place in the mid-nineties. What I remember most vividly is standing on the observation deck at the New York Stock Exchange, fascinated by the place. For a guy who dreamed of being a trader, this was it. Remember, this was years before computers took over trading. I looked out at the sea of traders—churning, roaring, frenetic—and the market muscle on full display.

I was twenty years old. I turned to Marty and said, "I need to do this. I'm going to get down here and do this somehow."

"Go for it," Marty said quietly.

But I had no clue that I was going to be one of those guys, that one day I would trade 9 percent of the volume of stocks in the S&P 500, nor that I would ring the bell to open trading in roughly twenty years' time.

TWO

UNLEASHING DIFFERENT

CHAPTER SIX
RUNNING FOR A SEAT IN PARLIAMENT

My friend Alex Baker was the first person I told that I was going to run for a seat in Canada's federal parliament. I rolled into class and we chatted as usual. "What's new?" he asked. "I'm going to run for Parliament," I said. I had gotten pretty involved with the York University Progressive Conservative club. Since the PCs hadn't had a shot at winning our local riding (a riding is the Canadian equivalent of a district in the U.S.) for the last fifty-odd years, the party was looking for a young kid who wanted some experience.

The nomination itself was a simple act. I stuck my hand up and said, "I'll do it." My philosophy: when an opportunity arises, just do it and figure out the details later. Put yourself in situations where you can thrive. You're never going to find perfection. Good enough is good enough.

The timing was particularly good for me to run as a candidate for Parliament. A professors' strike had shut down York University. My logic was that even if the strike ended and classes resumed, I would learn more over six months in a federal campaign than I ever could in a semester of classes. I could always make up the course work afterwards, but these opportunities didn't come around very often. It ended up being one of the turning points in my life.

I convinced my neighbor and good friend Pete Komorowski to come on board as my campaign manager. Pete lived in room 701 in Tatham Hall Residence, and I had 702. He's one of the most street-smart guys you'll ever meet. He's also a character. When he moved in, he took the doors off his closet and put them under his bed. He stuck a full-sized fridge in there for beer and beef. He would buy a side of beef and barbecue all week long. Pete was very spur-of-the-moment. I came home from class one Monday evening at four, and he said he was just finishing his application for Harvard Business School's MBA program, it was due in the morning, and did I want to drive it down with him? He didn't have time to courier it and he couldn't fax it, so four of us piled into his Jeep Cherokee and off we went. We got to Boston after midnight, dropped off the application, spent the day looking around a snowy Boston, and made the ten-hour drive back to Toronto just in time to grab some breakfast, change, and get into class to give a presentation. That was Pete's style.

Fernando Pica ended up being the official agent for my campaign and later stood as best man at my wedding. Like me, Fernando, Neil van Eijk, and Steve Adler formed part of the York Progressive Conservatives, and together we were building the tiny riding association—the local organized party unit, like a precinct in the United States—with some other locals off-campus. I also got a lot of help from the crew at the business school: Emmanuel Fenili, Paul Montgomery, Kien Ngyeun, and Kent Bailey.

Canada's House of Commons is one of two bodies that make up Parliament. Three hundred thirty-eight members of Parliament, one from each riding, are elected to the House by the people of Canada. The other body is called the Senate, to which 105 Senators are appointed until their retirement at seventy-five.

When I ran for Parliament, the federal PCs had just recently been decimated when Prime Minister Chrétien's Liberals swept to power. Only two PC members of Parliament remained: Jean Charest and Elsie Wayne. We were still a national party, but officially they called it a "rump" party. It was an interesting time to be part of a new beginning, a phoenix rising from the ashes. I had been interested in politics for probably ten years at that point, but this was the first time that I was officially part of the machine.

First task? I traveled to Ottawa for the party's five-day boot camp, where they drill you on the party platform, put you through team- and skill-building exercises, and help you to understand who you are as a speaker and as a media personality. We learned how a campaign is structured and how to build a team. At that time, Parliament held 301 seats, so 301 teams needed to be built. Five days was a very brief time to take all of this in, but it was important. When you're a candidate, you're not a name on a sign. You represent a national brand. Theoretically that's easy to understand, but until you're in the thick of it, you don't really know what it means.

So I arrived in Ottawa, a twenty-two-year-old kid surrounded by giants. There were probably thirty or forty of us new candidates in a downtown Ottawa hotel. Major-General Lewis MacKenzie, the former leader of the UN peacekeeping force in Bosnia-Herzegovina, and Peter MacKay, now former federal minister of justice, were both running for the first time. MacKay was my age—we kidded each other about the difficulties of running for Parliament at twenty-two—but he went on to win his riding and a successful tenure as one of Canada's leaders in Cabinet.

How am I going to compete with these guys? I asked myself. A lot of them had spent years training themselves on media techniques. I had never groomed myself to do this, but I threw myself into it. I had been doing it as an amateur for five or six years in student government, but I had never put my name on a sign outside of a school. This was a different animal. It was about issues like the economy, the justice system, immigration—issues that were hugely important to everyday Canadians. Of course, most voters don't elect a policy. They elect an individual. So a candidate has to come across as likeable and human, not just somebody who understands the Canadian mindset. I knew I couldn't come off as a policy wonk. I had to connect with my audience. So finding my voice and figuring out how to project not only my stance on various policy issues, but also my connections to those policies, was a real eye-opener.

I was surprised to learn that my speech impediment was, in this case, actually an asset. My wife, Jenn, talks about a speech I gave at Goldman Sachs years ago to candidates applying for summer internships. There were four of us on the panel, and she was in the back, observing. She said that when I spoke, the whole room seemed to lean forward, kind of lift out of their chairs to listen carefully. Because when I speak, people have to listen in order to understand what I say. Where I used to think that I had to adjust my speech so that others could understand, I now know that I have to let that go and use it as an asset. And it's a powerful one. I find that if someone listens to me for a couple minutes, they'll get it. You have to get used to my speech in the way you would get used to someone with a foreign accent. Within a brief time, people understand pretty clearly what the hell I'm saying. For TV, we figured out that we needed to use captioning. The Canadian Broadcasting Corporation captions all my interviews, and it seems to work pretty well. If I ever have to do live TV, I've decided to cross that bridge when I come to it.

In our world it's incredibly difficult to break through the noise unless you've got something unique. I've got something that's naturally different, and I have learned to use that to my advantage. When I speak I use slides that back up what I'm saying and give people cues. It takes a couple of slides to get into the speech pattern, but once they're into it, everything gets easier.

The experts in that candidates' school, the ones who do this for a living, told me that I came across as genuine, sincere, and honest. Which was probably because I'd had no coaching. I was just saying what I thought, saying what I felt in a way that I thought most people could understand. Over the years I have polished myself, but even then it was a very powerful, conversational style. It wasn't packaged—I would rather not try to become something that I wasn't. I learned that what came naturally to me was already a strength. Those lessons still impact me today. Now when I need to deliver a message to an audience, I take myself back to that candidates' school.

I learned from the other candidates as well. Major-General MacKenzie was particularly impressive. He was the star candidate that year, having just handed off command of the UN forces in Kosovo. There is a lot to be learned from a leader of men and women in danger. Observing the way that he handled various situations and projected leadership was immensely valuable to me as a young whippersnapper trying to figure it out for myself. Instead of acting like a big shot who owned the place, he became one of us. I guess he realized pretty quickly that people were looking to him for leadership. He was ultimately unsuccessful in his campaign, but watching him was a powerful lesson, and I'll never forget how he worked with the team of forty candidates, bonding us and bringing us together.

The PC Party held its campaign kickoff at the International Centre, out by the Toronto airport. By that time, I was already on the campaign trail, doing interviews and knocking on doors.

As part of the kickoff, all PC candidates got up on stage with the leader of the party, Jean Charest. This was just before Charest got screwed: in 1998, Prime Minister Chrétien would suggest that Charest was the best man to lead Quebeckers away from the idea of separation and would handpick him to lead the Liberal Party in Quebec. (At the time, a conflict over cultural identity had led to a Brexit-type event: some Quebeckers strongly wanted to separate from Canada in order to preserve and protect French culture. This separatist movement had formed its own political party during the 1960s and grown to great influence. Provincial referendums failed to endorse Quebec independence.) The switch from federal PC to provincial Liberal wasn't a big ideological shift for Charest, but it was a coup for Chrétien because it took Charest, the rising star of federal politics, out of the picture. I believe that, had he stayed, he would have been elected prime minister in at least one federal election, likely two.

It wasn't until the stage was fully set up and Charest was en route to the convention that we realized the organizers hadn't put up a ramp. I don't think anybody knew that I was coming with a scooter, and back in those days, building in accessibility just wasn't part of everyday planning like it is today. It was amusing to us, because we hadn't thought of it either. My team and I simply showed up with a scooter, not thinking about the seven-foot rise and how we were going to get the scooter onstage. So, as we did on many occasions back then, we used brute force. Six guys lifted me, scooter and all, onto the stage. My campaign manager, Pete, overheard one of the media guys saying, "This campaign's really going to start with a bang."

Because I was running in York West, I was the last candidate to be introduced—alphabetically by riding name. I had met Mr. Charest once before at candidate school, very briefly, when he signed my nomination papers. When you're introduced onstage, you're supposed to walk up to center stage, shake the man's hand, pose for a picture, wave to the crowd, and all that good stuff. When I rolled up to center stage from the back, and we were shaking hands, Mr. Charest leaned in and said, "I have been watching your campaign very closely in Ottawa. Anything you need, just give me a call personally. We know you have a tough fight, but we want to support you in every way possible." And for me, taking the leap that I did, with my team of newbies flinging themselves into the fray, what he said set me at ease and allowed me to focus on the task at hand, which was getting as many votes as possible.

One of the main techniques for doing that is meeting constituents face to face, which always involves knocking on doors. That hasn't changed for hundreds of years. Sure, there are media appearances and lawn signs and events to attend, but that is only part of getting elected. The larger parts are the strategic and tactical things that the team puts into place to get voters to actually cast a ballot. That's a science. I had not seen that side of politics before. There are processes to electioneering that are adjusted every cycle based on technology and the demographics of the voters. It's fascinating. But knocking on thirty thousand doors is still key. You need to establish a personal connection, and the best way to do that is person-to-person.

I learned a lot knocking on doors, running as a Conservative in one of the most Liberal ridings in the nation. Introducing myself, trying to convince lifelong Liberals to vote for me, was quite a hurdle to jump. The key was to remember that all politics is local. You're not going to run in a riding like York West on a bombastically conservative message. You're going to do a lot of listening; you're going to take in people's stories and anecdotes and try to relate them to your vision for the country. And we had a vision for the country. Our message at the door was "Let's get government out of your life to give you a shot at grabbing the brass ring."

I believe that most Canadians, most people in general, want

that. York West is full of hard-working middle-class people who are trying to get ahead every day of their lives. My message to those folks was "Hey, I get it, I want to help you get ahead. We have a platform that will do that." But most of what I did was listen. I think that good politicians, good leaders, know when to be quiet and take in information to better understand their audience. To use a business analogy, if you're in a sales meeting and you've done most of the talking, you're probably not going to make a sale. Because you don't know what the hell the customer wants. Whether your customer is a company, a consumer, or a voter, a customer is a customer is a customer. It doesn't matter what hat they wear. You're trying to earn their money, you're trying to earn their vote, you're trying to earn their trust. Your job is to shut up, listen, and try to meet their needs.

Knocking on doors wasn't all roses. Sometimes you would get to the door and you would have an older lady with her cane threatening to beat the crap out of you if you didn't get off her lawn, shouting that no conservative would ever cross her threshold. You'd get people blaming you because their brother was dying and couldn't access health care appropriately. A leader's job is to take that. I think most leaders fail when they get defensive. Never try to fight a voter on a point. Fight your opponent. But fight them with what your voters say, not with what *you* say. As a leader, you are only a vehicle.

In the end, I think two people kicked me out of their yards. Canadians tend to listen. I wasn't coming at them with the used-car salesman routine; I was relatively low risk to them. I don't believe in hardball politics. I think there are times for that, but they are few and far between. People usually want to have an honest conversation. If I did it over again, I probably would have knocked on more doors. Because I'm pretty good at the door. I'm pretty good at making that connection. There was one catch: we were limited in how much door-to-door campaigning I could do by the charge in the battery in my scooter—thankfully, scooter batteries last longer than human batteries.

I can't stress how important the connection is. Politics is incredibly personal. If you have actually met someone, chances are much higher that they will vote for you. Very few people vote based on ideology. They vote based on a connection to an individual. They form a personal connection with you; there is emotion tied up in the encounter; they're going to tell their friends that they met you; they will ultimately associate you with their main political interests. If you don't knock on a lot of doors, you're missing out. If you go to the door with a mask on, people will see right through it. If you go to the door as yourself and you're actually trying to connect, leaving yourself open and vulnerable, most people will reward you. Some won't—and you've got to learn how to cut those people off pretty quickly—but most people will reward you for it. A personal connection is what they crave, and that's very hard to manufacture.

People also vote by process of elimination. They vote against something. You have to figure out how to be acceptable, how to not get eliminated. It's a natural check and balance. If you don't do what people want you to do, they will turf you. If you do what they want you to do, they will keep you around. That can be on an issue-by-issue basis, it can be on a broad-spectrum basis where you do a little bit of everything well, or it can be the opposite, where you do a little bit of everything poorly. You can screw something up so massively that it tarnishes everything else, or you can be so lackluster on everything that people say, "I'm done."

In York West I was running against Sergio Marchi, the sitting minister of international trade. He was popular in the riding, but he wasn't exactly known for his nice-guy politics. We had our first all-candidates debate in a high school gym on Finch Avenue at Jane Street. I thought I was in for a fight. The room was packed, and I was uber-prepared. I had spent days getting ready for this.

I knew most of the policy ins and outs; I knew what the guy had voted on; I was ready to fight this guy tooth and nail. The NDP candidate was irrelevant. When I got up to speak, the first thing I said was "Sergio's got the easiest job in the room. He knows he's going to win. He's got to stay above the fray. My job is to drag him into the fray." I knew I had the room right there. The people who were engaged were already laughing.

It was a fun event. I nailed Marchi on every point, but he took it with good grace. It was a one-way fight—he knew he had his riding sewn up, and so did everyone else. I discovered that Marchi wasn't a policy whiz. He was the minister of trade for Canada, and he would have real struggles to calculate a trade surplus. As the debate wore on, I became more and more incredulous. I was like, *Wow, is this real? Canada's minister of trade is getting schooled by a twenty-two-year-old kid?* The whole campaign was a realization for me. *Wait a sec*, I thought. *I can run circles around one of Canada's leaders—a guy who is supposed to be driving our country's future, and I'm able to outpace him.* That made me realize that these were just people and not always particularly clever ones at that. I left that campaign thinking, *Hell, if they can do it, I can do it.* There is no magic to success. It's just taking a risk, providing great content, and delivering it with some pizzazz. If I was able to give these guys a run for their money, then anything is possible.

I learned that when meeting people I'd never met before—people who have hopes and dreams of their own—I had to find a way to frame those hopes and dreams as realistic and doable. That's a leader's job—to make anything possible in other people's minds. Whether you're coaching a sports team, leading a business unit, leading a campaign team, or speaking to millions of people, a leader charts a course and paints a picture of the world, inviting others to believe in that picture. I think people often mistake leadership for execution. Leaders don't execute visions. There just aren't enough hours in the day to do that. They project visions.

They paint pictures. They stretch people. You can't stretch and do at the same time. Any good leader needs a team to go execute and to shape, adjust, and tweak that vision to make it a reality.

As the campaign drew to a close, I was preoccupied with ensuring that the campaign team knew that their efforts weren't wasted. We all went in knowing that it was in fact a sacrificial-lamb campaign, but nonetheless my team was composed of people in their early twenties who were used to winning. We were all very high achievers; we were a group of people who wanted to learn and to be innovative in the political process. In 1997, ours was one of the first campaigns anywhere to put an email address on campaign signs and literature. But it was also a campaign that was going to have a different ending than we were used to. So well before it was over, I made sure that I went out of my way to thank people, to make sure that they got the experiences that they wanted to get. I'm still pretty close with all of those people today.

On election night, we all gathered in our campaign headquarters—a former ice cream shop in a strip mall that we got for free because it was a space awaiting a retrofit between leases. We had posters and streamers up, and Pete got a side of beef and barbecued for everyone that came by. As for myself, I had never been so terrified. And I don't scare easily. I was sick to my stomach. That was the first time I'd put my name on the line for anything. And because of what I am, I'm easily recognizable. Midway through the campaign, City-TV did a story on me that got a lot of play, and as a result, when we traveled around Toronto, people would yell, "Hey, Rich, good luck!" That made it even tougher both for me and for my team. I wanted to have a good showing. My team had sacrificed a lot of time and energy to help build a legitimate campaign. When you're at that point, you're thinking, *Are we going to get, like, fifty votes?* The way I was thinking was *Okay. I know I'm going to get at least three votes: I voted for myself, Pete voted for me, and Fernando voted for me.* I was petrified of being embarrassed. I didn't want to embarrass the party; I didn't want to embarrass the people who had worked very hard for me. And it was my name on the sign. I didn't want to go down as the guy who got fifty votes.

We rigged up a TV at the HQ and watched the results trickle in. What do you know, but ours was the first return that came up for Ontario. They had "Richard Donovan in the lead with 100 votes to 13." We just started laughing. It was such a relief. I remember thinking, *Okay. At least one hundred people voted for us.*

When the final results came in, I realized that I could have won that campaign. Especially in light of my debate with Marchi. What had seemed a dream was actually relatively simple to do. We ultimately got 2,165 votes out of just under 29,000. That seems like a small number, but I was a total newbie running against a nationally known politician. It was respectable.

This wasn't like climbing Mount Everest. I saw that there were things I could have done to win the election. I learned then that every fight is winnable. If you're in a fight that's unwinnable, don't fight. That was the last time I remember planning to lose anything. I didn't understand that going in, but I did coming out. My horizon went from about five inches off the floor to vertical. I just started to think in terms of *Well, if we can do that, why can't we do this?*

Those seven months set up the next eighteen years. My lesson to others is this: if you can think it, you can do it. You've got to take that first step and be comfortable saying, "I'm going to get into this. I don't know how I'm going to do it, but I'll figure it out when I get there." There is no straight line to success. The most successful person in the history of the world is just a person. Nothing magical, no pixie dust; they just decided to go.

It was because of that campaign that I met David Onley, a gentleman I still count as a friend. I got a phone call one morning at five, or rather my campaign manager did. A producer said, "Hey, can Rich do an interview with City-TV today?" He didn't know that I had a disability—he was just doing candidate profiles.

At that point David was a reporter at City-TV, doing mostly science and technology news and weather. He covered some politics as well, but that wasn't his primary beat. So he came up to York for the interview, and we had a great chat. We've stayed connected ever since. When David became lieutenant governor of Ontario, Her Majesty the Queen's representative in the province, I was one of his unofficial advisers. When you're in a role like that, you need advisers you can call and say, "Hey, what do you think about this?" I played that role for David on the disability side, and we've kept up a good friendship.

I took a page out of his book in learning to handle disability. When Moses Znaimer—best known as the founder of a large independent Toronto-based media business—interviewed him for the reporter job at City-TV, he asked if the disability thing was going to affect how David did his job. (David had polio as a child, has issues walking, and prefers to use a scooter.) David said precisely this: "I don't know. We'll figure it out."

When I got to Wall Street, I got asked the same thing, and I gave the same answer. I think what happens in boardrooms and in meeting rooms trumps all of this theoretical disability "playbooks and best practice" that you get from governments and legal experts. The world doesn't work in a vacuum. It doesn't look at the statutes. It doesn't work academically. These are real businesses run by human beings who have to get real stuff done. If you're not willing to have an open conversation, well, there is not going to be a hell of a lot of trust built up between you and the person on the other side of the desk.

Much later, after I graduated from Columbia Business School, I was interviewing for a job where eventually I would be handling billions of dollars in capital. There were some obvious questions that the hiring manager sitting across from me didn't ask, because the law says that you can't. Regardless, if you're going to build up the trust required to feel good about someone, there has to be an open, honest conversation at some point. It's hard to walk around a room with an elephant in it. Elephants take up a lot of space, they smell, they move around, they bump you every now and again. It's better to deal with them quickly. I think that's what we forget when we get into this ubiquitous legal conversation about requirements and accommodations. This isn't a theoretical world. And in my experience, at least, the questions and barriers go away very quickly when you have a real conversation and develop some trust.

CHAPTER SEVEN
MY INTRODUCTION TO PUBLIC FINANCE

W hen the election was over and school was done, I was a junior analyst at Citi, trying to figure out what was next. I desperately wanted to get more experience that would prepare me to be a trader, so I decided to look around for jobs in Toronto.

Why was being a trader so appealing to me? A trader buys and sells securities with two goals: to manage short-term risk and to make a profit for his or her clients. I believe in the power of fair markets to reward the best ideas, the best companies, and the best deals. Becoming a trader is the ultimate in working with markets, just as reaching the major leagues is the ultimate in playing baseball. And not to mention—I process math problems pretty damn quickly.

So what happens during a trade? Hypothetically, let's say IBM is due to report its earnings tomorrow. The consensus among experts and investors is that it will miss its earnings forecast—in other words, its business performance has not been as good as it predicted.

The trader has an opportunity to buy, sell, or do nothing with the IBM stock, based on what she believes will happen with the earnings announcement the next day. The trader assesses the risk of different scenarios. Will IBM surprise the market with a better-than-expected number? That scenario suggests holding on to her position or buying more, because she can sell IBM stock the next day for a higher price than she bought it at. Or will IBM miss its estimate by even more than expected? Is this negative view spreading on Wall Street? That scenario suggests selling IBM today before its price falls, or shorting the stock, which means assessing that the stock will fall in price and positioning to gain from that event without already owning the stock. There are many ways to do this. Another scenario: the stock won't move much. The trader could sit on her position for a while longer or provide a way for others to create positions that are different than hers—at a price, of course. Traders take positions on their judgment of how markets and investors will behave. Half economist, half predictive psychologist.

Becoming a trader was a chance to make money for clients and the firm, using my talents and passion for market dynamics. So I put the word out within my political and university networks that I was looking for a market risk or trading job at a Canadian financial institution. The first thing that came up was an opening for a risk analyst at the Ontario Financing Authority (OFA). The OFA is the closest thing that the Province of Ontario has to a central bank. The OFA issues bonds, buys and sells derivatives to manage that debt, educates institutional investors on what's going on with provincial finances, and acts as a financial adviser for the government of Ontario.

Municipal, state, provincial, and federal government agencies raise money by issuing bonds that investors purchase knowing they will earn a return of interest on their investment. A bond pays the investor back with interest over time. In nations such as Canada and the United States, these bonds are viewed by the markets as having a minimal risk of failure; therefore, the issuing agency can pay lower interest rates to investors than some corporate bonds. Government bonds are considered "safe," and some are tax-protected—you earn your interest profit without paying certain taxes.

I had my first interview at OFA with the director of market risk, Doug Harrington. I was offered a position as a risk analyst and was soon taking the train to Toronto's Union Station downtown and the subway up to the OFA offices at the Eaton Centre tower at Dundas and Yonge. The job was a nice combination of public policy and finance—that was my thinking going into it. I didn't realize that because it was a small shop, I would get the chance to do things that I would never get to do at a big bank so early in my career. I quickly gained direct exposure to traders, financial engineers (typically mathematicians, engineers, or computer scientists who use computer models to run simulations to assess risk and profit for a client's requested result), and intelligent people who understood how bonds and financial markets worked.

The market risk department, which I had recently joined, was responsible for minimizing the cost of borrowing for Ontario. We had purview over OFA's portfolio and looked at things one would typically find in a market risk scenario, such as the impact of interest rate fluctuations to the outstanding debt of the Province of Ontario—Canada's largest provincial economy. If we had to borrow, we wanted to do it at the lowest cost possible. The added twist was that, unlike a bank, we had a public policy element as well. We had to consider how what we did would change the province's long-term financial position. When I left in July 2000 to attend Columbia Business School, the provincial debt was about CDN$35 billion. When I returned to Toronto in late 2014, the debt had ballooned above CDN$300 billion. In other words, it took fourteen years to explode the debt to eight times the level that was issued over the previous 133 years. One word comes to mind—wow. Yes, that is my technical financial assessment.

It was the best of both worlds: exposure to managing a large portfolio of bonds, plus insight into how government operations impact government budgets and their ability to achieve goals via finance. I learned that seeing how a "central bank" operates is basically like looking under the hood of the economy; you see where cash flows go in the public books (say, to a major capital building project like a bridge), how that cash is used (to finance the capital building project), and how it benefits investors and taxpayers (a new bridge). As I would later learn at Columbia, cash flow is everything to an organization. Knowledge of cash flow would change how I looked at the world from an economic and a policy point of view.

At the ripe old age of twenty-three, I was a risk analyst charged with running the OFA's daily risk reports. That was more difficult than it sounds, because at the time we did it using Excel. It was like trying to keep a 1950s roadster in top condition over the course of a five-hundred-lap race. That time, around 1998–99, was the peak of the internet bubble, and it was also a transition period between custom-built and off-the-shelf financial solutions. We couldn't find anything off-the-shelf that would run our computations, so our team had built risk models using good old Excel.

Working in Excel forced me to get into the weeds. I had looked at risk portfolios before but had never actually built them. I worked closely with John Logie, a financial engineer who built the system we were using—a very smart guy who had written his Ph.D. thesis on the pricing of milk. John taught me a lot about asset pricing. He hammered home how to use the mechanisms of risk. If you understand the language of risk, you understand finance and you understand price. I can price your shoelaces based on the risks involved in making them and getting them to you. I just can't tie them for you.

During the late 1990s, the dot-com bubble was inflating the stock markets. Anyone who got into the tech stock market was making money for a while. Cabbies and barbers were trading and making hundreds of thousands of dollars. I was doing well with my own personal trading. So while the world was drinking the dot-com Kool-Aid, I was being grounded in risk. It was another way the job was perfect for me at the time.

The OFA trading floor was small but well appointed, and our traders each managed a book of debt on which the province actively managed financial risks to minimize costs to the taxpayer. The OFA issued short-term bonds, medium-term ten-year bonds, and long-term thirty-year bonds. We managed the risk attached to each by hedging with derivatives. Derivatives are deals based on stocks, bonds, or commodity prices like oil, where their value is determined by fluctuations in the underlying asset over time. Each side of a trade is positioned for what happens to the price of that asset in the future as influenced by economic and other external events. These instruments are used as a way of hedging risk, because you can gain exposure that covers the upside and downside of the price of an asset. Investors use derivatives to protect themselves against prices going the wrong way. Think of them as insurance—likely not needed but usually a smart thing to have.

Now, I'm differentiating between large investors and outright speculation. Like any tool, derivatives can be used to create value, and they can be used to destroy value. Derivatives get a bad reputation as the cause of various financial crises. Tools don't cause crises, people do. Poor risk management was at the core of the 2008 financial apocalypse. Not greed. Not stupidity. The U.S. portfolio management system was poorly measuring and managing risk. Okay, "poorly" may be an understatement.

I was invited by OFA's risk team to join them on a major project to reinvent how OFA priced its bonds and derivatives. The mission involved developing mathematical models and software that would assess with high accuracy the risk factors for a bond at any point in time. Twenty years beforehand, we would have computed the long-form mathematics using calculators and notepads to calculate how future interest rates would unfold.

I can remember leading the team in brainstorming the approach. We spent a few days in the boardroom, trying to figure out how our new price model would work. So here I was, fresh out of school, leading a team of Ph.D.s in a brainstorming session. That facilitation became a blueprint for what would become a routine first step in anything I took on later. My job was to facilitate, not to add value as a participant.

I said to the team, "Look at me as the UN. When we're in this room, I'm on no one's side, but I'm the boss. For this to work, I have to manage it." You can just imagine it, this twenty-three-year-old kid playing tough guy with seven or eight Ph.D.s in the room. The big boss, Kanak Chopra, said, "Oh, you're the boss now, are you?" And I said, "Just for the next two hours, yeah." Kanak was director of risk control. One of the nicest guys you'll ever meet, smart as a whip.

One friend of mine at OFA was Jean-François Marleau. Jean-François, or J-F to his colleagues, was a well-dressed French-Canadian from Montreal with a deep background in risk who shared my love of hockey. He was an easygoing guy with a great sense of humor and a talent for being blunt and to the point. Jean-François and I went to a Leafs-Canadiens game in Montreal one weekend. We drove down Friday after work, I stayed with my cousin, and we partied in Montreal for the weekend. The Leafs won the game. This was before 2004, pre-lockout. Back in those days I used to go to a lot of Leafs games because I could always count on getting wheelchair seats—they never sold out. I picked the cheap seats, which were \$35 as opposed to \$120, and they were just as good.

I collaborated with two other people at OFA quite a bit, Pauline Lai and Iris Ko. They were wonderful mentors. Pauline, Iris, and Jean-François brought me up to speed quickly. They helped me to understand the nuances of pricing securities, to understand how risk affects cash flows, and how to look at everything from a public finance perspective. They were just good, fun people. Pauline was, and still is, a leader in terms of both knowledge and her ability to show people the way ahead. As the senior risk analyst, she knew where the holes were, she knew where the bodies were buried. Iris was like Pauline. She had a profound sense of humor. She was a leader, a little bit of a lighter touch than Pauline, but incredibly smart and knowledgeable about mathematics and risk.

The thing I remember about all three of those people is that their doors were always open. They made a concerted effort to teach. I think they saw that as part of their duty. And a lot of the time, I was the beneficiary. I think it's a rare thing for a young kid to be exposed to an environment where you can learn as much as you want. The whole ecosystem was wired to teach, and I made the most of it. I was at a point in my life where all I wanted to do was learn.

At the same time as I was doing my day job, I was completing my preparation to take the chartered financial analyst (CFA) certification. When you prep for the CFA you're basically studying thirty hours a week from February to June, so between that and my job at the OFA, I was working my butt off. For two years, I would get to work around eight, leave work around six, and study a couple of hours a night. It was a lot of work, but it was worth it.

The OFA job was important to my later trading career because it trained me in the basics of risk on the debt side. Most equity traders have no exposure to fixed income instruments. The equity guys look at the bond guys as wonks; the bond guys look at the equity guys as a mile wide and an inch deep. The reality is that equity is far more complex than debt because there are more variables involved. The way I look at it, debt is more of a science; equity is more of a craft. There is a touch and a feel to equity that really doesn't exist on the fixed income side, where you're ruled by the almighty yield curve. That's the big driver. That's also your constraint. On the equity side, you're ruled by both earnings and interest rates. The variables that go into earnings are far greater than the variables that go into interest rates. Credit ratings are key on the debt side too, especially when things go bad. However, when things go bad, debt looks a lot like equity.

The OFA job allowed me to punch way above my weight. And it paid okay; it allowed me to get my first car and enjoy life. The car I leased was a silver 1999 Mercury Cougar. Brand-new. I chose it because it was different. The '99 was a uniquely styled car, almost like a fighter jet. It was a little bit outside the norm but still affordable. The Cougar was lighter than a Honda Civic and came with a V6 engine. The thing flew. Earning enough to lease a car was a bonus, but the pay wasn't why I was there. Had I known what the job entailed when I signed up, I would have done it for next to nothing. You don't get jobs like that when you're twenty-three. It just doesn't happen.

CHAPTER EIGHT
COLUMBIA CALLING

At the end of my second year at the OFA, I was applying to MBA programs at Ivy League schools. At the top of my list, of course, was Columbia. I had been wait-listed at Columbia because my GMAT scores were low. As I mentioned earlier, I have always tested poorly because the logistics of written testing aren't a good fit. I saw this problem as just part of having to be better than my competition because of what the mainstream saw as limitations.

I did some research on how to get off the wait list. I realized if I did nothing, I was going to stay on the wait list forever. But if I made the admissions team believe that I really wanted it, they would admit me. So that's what I did. I phoned and I emailed and I phoned some more. I did whatever I could.

An alumni interview was part of the process. My interviewer was a guy named Steve Mayer who worked at the Toronto office of Morgan Stanley. I bought a new suit for the interview. I decided to try something new: I bought blue silk suspenders, the color of Columbia. I had this uniform I was wearing that I thought was awesome. It just made me feel like a million bucks. Steve and I hit it off, and I nailed the interview. This was before I was wait-listed; once I was put on the wait list and realized I needed to "fight my way in," I called Steve. He said, "I'll put the word in for you as well. We'll put the full court press on the admissions team, get you off the wait list and get you in."

That was early May 2000. A week later, I was sitting at my desk at the OFA on a gorgeous spring day. I was minding my business, doing my work, starting to think about what I wanted to eat for lunch. I had already been admitted to the University of Western Ontario's MBA program. Just that morning on my way to work, I had gone to the bank and dropped a money order for the registration fee for Western in the mailbox. I was still focused on making it to New York, but I had to cover my bases, and Western is a great school. I was excited to be moving onto a new path.

Then I got a phone call. "Rich, it's Linda Meehan, director of admissions at Columbia. How are you doing today?"

"Good. How are you doing?"

"Great. I have a question for you, Rich. If I admit you to Columbia Business School, will you come?"

"I would accept on the spot," I said.

"Congratulations. You are the newest member of the Class of 2002."

My head exploded with joy. I had never felt that good in my life. Once I got off the phone, I literally screamed "Holy crap!" and did a little dance. I yelled, "I think I got into Columbia! No, I *know* I just got into Columbia! I'm going to Columbia Business School!"

That's a moment that I will never forget. It's one of the happiest of my life because I knew what it meant. I didn't really understand where it would take me, but I knew it was a life-changing moment.

I remember driving home that evening. It was mid-May, I had the windows down, the sunroof open. The tunes were cranked. I had achieved a goal that I had set eight years earlier, when I was sixteen, and now I could put this goal to bed. I'm going to a top business school and I'm getting my shot at Wall Street.

When the euphoria died down, reality hit. How I was going to pay for it? We were middle class and my parents did well, but they never saved for our schooling. Right off the bat, my dad assuaged my fears. He said, "Rich, don't worry about it, just accept the offer. We'll figure that out later." He was right: I had an unbelievable opportunity in front of me, and I had to take it.

I learned that as a Columbia Business School student, I had access to every bank on Wall Street. I could pick up the phone and call an alum, and even if they didn't recruit me, that alum would meet with me. Today, I answer those calls, even when I don't know who they're from. If you're a Columbia Business School alum, you get access to me. Full stop. We're connected by a series of shared experiences. I think that those most attached to the school are the ones whose lives it changed the most. For me, the change was huge. I went from a network that was topping out in Canada and stretching into politics to an instantaneous global network. As a graduate, I have colleagues in most countries in the world. One of the things schools in the U.S. have developed better than anywhere else is fostering and maintaining that alumni network. Canada doesn't do that well at all—we don't have the same attachment to our schools.

Columbia Business School's great relationship with banks and financial institutions is based on the global reputation and history of its value investing program, which operates out of the Heilbrunn Center for Graham & Dodd Investing and is guided by Bruce Greenwald, an adviser to many top hedge fund managers and investors.

Value investing as a system was pioneered by investing giants Benjamin Graham and David Dodd, who began teaching at Columbia Business School in 1928 and subsequently developed an encyclopedia detailing their system in the 1934 (and frequently revised) text *Security Analysis*. Super-investor Warren Buffett, who got an A-plus from Benjamin Graham at Columbia in 1951, made his fortune using the principles of *Security Analysis*. Buffett penned a wonderful article for the Business School about a group of four students of Graham's who worked with him after graduation:

> I begin this study of results by going back to a group of four of us who worked at Graham-Newman Corporation from 1954 through 1956. There were only four—I have not selected these names from among thousands. I offered to go to work at Graham-Newman for nothing after I took Ben Graham's class, but he turned me down as overvalued. He took this value stuff very seriously! After much pestering, he finally hired me. There were three partners and four of us at the "peasant" level. All four left between 1955 and 1957 when the firm was wound up, and it's possible to trace the record of three.

The four peasants were Buffett, Walter Schloss, Tom Knapp, and Bill Ruane. They are all among the most successful investors of the past fifty years, posting astonishing returns. I mention value investing because it is so instrumental to Columbia's deserved stature with Wall Street and fund managers globally. My classmate Todd Combs is one of Warren Buffett's portfolio managers and is positioned as a part of the succession plan at Berkshire Hathaway. I had the opportunity to study with the value investing faculty, and it was an incredible opportunity. While I was more focused on the quantitative approach, the deep dive on cash flow would be the base of my thinking as a portfolio manager.

The Business School offers so many great professors who are winning major awards and wonderfully dedicated to teaching. I was enormously grateful to be admitted and learn from them, but let me be clear: if you are interested in attending a graduate or business school and don't get admitted to your first choice, many other programs offer their own stellar faculties, networks, connections, and education. You will find the best fit for your plans and abilities. Don't be afraid to use every ethical advantage at your disposal, including if you are classified technically or by the world as "different." That was something I finally learned in the Columbia process.

In my admissions essay, I portrayed my disability as an asset. It was the first time I had addressed disability in a professional way and the first time I had portrayed it in a positive light. I had learned that my disability wasn't a problem for admissions; it was an advantage. I had been going to MBA fairs and talking with the admissions directors of U.S. business schools who told me, "Look, you have a different profile. That's attractive to us. We like having a mix at our school."

I used a rocket ship analogy in my admissions essay, writing that "I face additional forces, so I need to be more powerful and more aerodynamic than every other rocket." I had been using that concept to motivate myself for a long, long time. But that was really the first time that I can recall when I voiced the thought publicly. I talked about my disability in my admissions applications not just for the sake of getting into the school of my choice but also to show how I used it to my advantage, and I talked about it in a way that was real and true.

I realized that if my disability was an asset when it came to admissions, I needed to portray it an asset in business as well. I succeeded. I'm still selling myself. As a Canadian, I'm rare in that respect; we don't do that very well. Americans are trained to sell themselves from day one. But to be honest, dogged persistence is what got me into Columbia. I wanted to be there, I wanted it badly. I think that was plainly evident to the school.

I kept my job at the OFA until the first week of July. I took a couple weeks off, but it was hardly a vacation. I had just finished the test for level two of the CFA, I had been preparing for the move to New York since May, and I was exhausted. I was about to move to a new city, a new country, and live hundreds of miles from home for the first time in my life, essentially without a support system. I had some work to do. I had to figure out immigration, I had to figure out where I was going to live, I had to figure out what I was going to do for furniture, what I was going to do for clothes, and take care of silly things like getting a social security number.

I was doing this with what others consider to be a significant disability. My perception of added "difficulty" is different than most, simply because these methods and paths are all I know. I think of the added difficulty in terms of low double digits when it's probably triple digits. It's probably 100 percent, 200 percent, or 400 percent harder for me to do certain things than for most people. Take something as simple as walking down the street. When I walk, my brain is already thinking about fifty steps ahead. I think real fast. I walk real slow. It doesn't frustrate me—it's what I do. But most people would just friggin' walk it, or run it, depending on how quickly they wanted to get where they were going. But when I walk, I'm using what feels like every muscle in my body to do four discrete things: balance, move forward, aim, and make it look like it's under control.

In my brain, I'm doing these things knowing that there is no expectation of precision. Walking is the thing that I'm least confident doing and is likely the most complex thing I do—including managing a portfolio. There are 640 muscles in your body, and I use most of them to walk. For me, walking is more will than skill. No pain, but if you're trying to have a deep conversation with me on my feet, be set for brevity.

Sometimes, I fall. Like most people with CP, I am an expert at taking a knee safely and getting myself up. It's no big deal.

Some people ask what my life would be like if I wasn't disabled, as in, "You have done very well; without a disability, you'd probably be the prime minister or Canada's top astronaut." If you have a disability, I don't need to tell you: life doesn't work that way. To assess what your life would be without disability is to try and prove a negative. What I know for sure: if I wasn't disabled, I wouldn't be doing what I am doing today.

I would probably be some guy who enjoys hockey way more than he should. I might be a pilot. Something—anything—that would never have led me to where I am now. I think the way to look at it is, if I didn't have a disability, I wouldn't have had the opportunities that I had. Full stop. "What if" is kind of a silly construct in the first place, and it means I'd be using somebody else's assessment of what's important. For instance, most people think that walking is important. But really, it's not. How you get from point A to point B doesn't matter too much. Still, there was a whole construct when I was a kid where they wanted to fix me, they wanted to make me walk straight. I can't think of a single instance in my life where walking in a straight line would have helped me. The other thing is, skills aren't additive. My biggest skill is the ability to take a concept and make it real. If I wasn't disabled, how much value would walking a straight line actually add? Maybe 1 or 2 percent, because I could get through an airport quicker? Actually, that's a bad example. I can usually get through an airport faster because I bypass the long security line.

Here's the analogy I use. Imagine you're in the movie *Back to the Future* and you go back in time to a decision point. If I were an able-bodied twelve-year-old kid, would I choose to go to a political rally or to play baseball? Probably baseball. Probably. Disability impacted my path and how I navigated the world. The choices I made and still make are profoundly impacted by my disability. I had an incredible advantage simply because I didn't look at the world in terms of "what if."

Because disability forced me to do mathematics in my head, it has cascaded into a set of assets that very few people have. But thanks to society's perception of disability, few people see that. People with disabilities often struggle with their own view of themselves based on society's perceptions because they've been told one thing their whole lives: "What if?" The what-if construct affects and infects a lot of perceptions in disability. I say to hell with what if!

A lot of able-bodied people see disability as a death sentence: *Oh boy, I could never do that. It must be terrible.* The reality is, it's not. For the bulk of people with disabilities, it doesn't define them. Not the way people think it does. Being disabled is not who they are.

About 20 percent of people around the world have a disability. You wouldn't know that, because the average person with a disability is not a poster child. The statistics say that the income of people with disabilities lags the average at a ratio of 100:91, not the 100:25 that people would have you believe. For many of you, the concept of disability conjures up mental images of a "severe," visible disability. That's one of the biggest problems for people facing disability. The folks with more involved disabilities have dominated the conversation. Those responsible are typically the parents of these individuals. They have used charities, and charities have used them, to paint a picture of what disability is for society. I can't blame them for it—they're just advocating for their son or daughter—but that picture puts many people dealing with a disability at a disadvantage.

In the same way, the business community has engaged with people with disabilities largely on a charitable basis: donate, host an event, organize an employee group, and you've done everything that you can. Legislation has forced hiring quotas, but that doesn't encourage companies to hire the best and the brightest, nor are the quotas anywhere near successful. What companies have missed is exceedingly simple: they must attract people with disabilities as customers to prove value to the organization. Delighting the customer must come first. The same process can be applied to all non-traditional markets, including those defined by gender, race, ethnicity, and sexual orientation. Delight the customer, and economic returns follow. The social goal of equal employment follows only as a symptom of intentional market success. In a way, I've been fighting my whole life to change this perspective, and you'll learn more about how we're making progress in part 3 of this book.

Probably the toughest conversations I have are with parents of kids who have serious issues with their disabilities and are not developing their potential. The parents have a lot to deal with and struggle mightily with things that most people take for granted. They want to fight for their kid. Which, as a parent, I *totally* get. We would do the same for our son, Maverick. But addressing disability solely from one's own experience is probably not the best approach to improving things for everyone grappling with disability. These voices can be so dramatic that they tend to suck all the air out of the room, so to speak. They obscure lots of other issues that can act as levers to generate opportunity for millions.

All people with disabilities hold the potential to be productive members of society. Consumers. Employees. Taxpayers. Will they all be rocket scientists and middle class or above? Of course not, but that is true for everyone, disability or not. We must learn to separate disability from other socioeconomic factors.

My job is to take a market-wide view and create a process driven by facts and data. It's a methodical, strategic way of changing things for many people with disabilities. Sometimes I find that difficult to do because, as a human being, you want to help these folks. You want to do whatever you can as an individual and as a society to make life easy. The problem is that the other 90 percent must walk out in society with that label around their neck. And that label doesn't reflect reality.

Of course, when I got the acceptance to Columbia, I didn't yet know that this would become my work of a lifetime. But I did know that something great was about to begin.

CHAPTER NINE

EMPIRE STATE OF MIND

O n Friday, August 4, 2000, Mom and I caught a plane to New York. It was the scariest time of her life, she would later tell my wife. She worried about how I would make out, how I would manage on my own in the Big Apple. She did a very good job of hiding that, which made for a fun weekend. It was surreal. What I had dreamed of for so long was happening. I was flinging myself into the breeze, confident that I could do it without knowing exactly how.

For me, that weekend was a thank you to Mom, to show her New York City and set her mind at ease. We stayed at the Hilton on Sixth Avenue, and I took her to dinner and a show on Saturday night. My parents had just taken out a second mortgage on the house to secure my loan to go to Columbia, so I was watching every dollar closely. Mom and I had to be at Columbia Housing on Monday, so we had two days to play tourist—Circle Line, Central

Park, Columbia campus—and enjoy NYC food. I remember the meals most fondly. In hindsight, I'm certain she was nervous, but our conversations were full of optimism, likely aided by one or two cocktails. I was terrified, but the weekend of acclimatization was exactly what I needed to calm my nerves.

On Sunday, my dad and brother met us with a big yellow Ryder truck at 119th and Morningside. It turned out to be the hottest day of the year. To move all that stuff into my building in the heat wasn't going to be easy, so we ended up hiring a guy off the street for fifty dollars to help us out. My family had brought the furniture I grew up with, along with a few particleboard additions, to Manhattan. It was a piece of Toronto in New York.

I had managed to get campus housing—Columbia is one of the largest real estate owners in New York City, but all the same I was lucky to get one of those apartments. I was paying $700 a month in rent when the market value was $3,000. It was quite a shock when I eventually left campus and had to get my own place.

I'm sure I got that apartment because Butler Hall was one of the few buildings Columbia owned that was wheelchair accessible. It was a grand building, a spectacular turn-of-the-century hotel that they had converted into an apartment building. It was classic old New York, with huge oak revolving doors.

When you walked into the lobby, you could imagine that you were back in the Prohibition era. There was a great mahogany front desk, a lobby full of rich earthy colors, old-fashioned fixtures, and lofty ceilings. I was quite fortunate to have that apartment. My kitchen was a closet with a sink and a hotplate in it, but the location was spectacular. I had a claw-foot tub, which I had never had before. I had to figure out how to get into and out of the thing without breaking my leg or bumping my head too many times. As my family headed back north, I was thinking, *Oh, right, I have to take a shower in this thing.* I'd had a walk-in shower in Toronto. It was just another one of those details that

I hadn't thought about when I moved. But I would find a way to make it work.

Then came orientation. I first met my classmates when we had what they call a cluster meeting. Clusters were groups of sixty students formed to create a support network for freshmen. We were Cluster B, and we were meeting on the third floor of Uris Hall. I was late, which for me is almost unheard of. I'm never late for anything. It's like a badge of honor. You can imagine the trepidation I was feeling, rolling into this amphitheater on my scooter with everybody already there.

I was fearful that people were looking at me and thinking, *What the hell is that?* I was nervous about competing at this level, at keeping up. My peers were very good at what they did and exceedingly smart. How the heck was I going to compete? I didn't know it at the time, but this was my new family. As a cluster, you're going to be learning together for a year. You're going to spend more time with these sixty people over the following ten months than you're going to spend with anybody. You don't know that at the time, but that's what's ahead of you.

Based on what I thought I knew about Ivy League MBA students, I was expecting to meet a bunch of type A a-holes. I couldn't have been more wrong. In an MBA class, you have a group of people with the same values, the same ambitions, and a similar level of achievement. That's a recipe for deep camaraderie. The reality is, you don't make it to that level if you're an a-hole. You get shot down before then. If you have gone through the hoops and gotten over the hurdles, you're probably a team player.

I discovered that I didn't have to do this on my own. Lots of people around me wanted me to succeed and went out of their way to make that possible. That included classmates, professors, administrators at the Business School, and staff at the university. I was wholly unprepared for that reality. I was ready for a fight—to compete. I had my back up. What I should have been preparing for was a deep bonding experience, personal growth, and relationship development.

I appreciate this even more now, because in looking back it's obvious that Columbia wasn't used to people like me. There weren't people with visible disabilities all over the place. I was blown away with the level of service that I got, and it's a good thing that I got it. What I was trying to do was not easy, and I could not have done it without a lot of help. I was so busy keeping up that I didn't really think about it, but now I know a lot of people were looking out for me. The entire community took me in so that I wouldn't be left out . . . ever.

Once I made the realization that I wasn't in for a colossal fight, things immediately got easier. It would have been nice to know that going in, but my brain was on red alert, all that fight-or-flight anxiety. Life tends to teach you lessons on its own time-table. That isn't to say that stress went away—I was far too busy for that to happen. Those days were so intense and dramatically different than what I had known. I was comfortable with the academic material, but the pace was new. The pace of New York City in general and Columbia Business School specifically was a hell of a lot quicker than I was used to. I remember being able to recall every detail of every hour of every day, which I think must be what it's like being on speed. Adapting to that new pace of life, that new speed of thought, changed the way that I thought about everything. I felt hypersensitive, super-aware. A lot of that was driven by those around me. They were faster, stronger, and I had to work hard to keep up.

My wheels helped me keep up—I didn't bring my car to New York. To get around, mostly I walk, with a wobble. But for speed and distance, I use a scooter. Very helpful in New York. I choose to use it because in certain instances I'm more productive. I even make it part of my identity. When I buy a scooter, I want it to have some style, some pizzazz. I want some height to it, I want to be able to look people straight in the eye. If it's going to become part of my identity, which is inevitable, I want it to look decent.

Like all New Yorkers, I have a love-hate relationship with the bustling streets. I love the energy and the unspoken knowledge that it takes resilient, savvy people to live here. Generally, people aren't going out of their way to help you (until you really need help), but they also don't judge you. It's a "suck it up, let's get it done" kind of place; but make no mistake, if I fall down, someone will extend a helping hand.

I learned to balance the total inaccessibility of the transportation system with the reality of owning the sidewalks on my scooter. I figured that since I grudgingly accepted the inaccessible infrastructure, I would not feel any qualms about asserting myself elsewhere. I paid enough taxes for a subway that I could not use, so being assertive with my three-hundred-pound scooter sat well with me.

When I rolled into the amphitheater a few minutes late, Cluster B had started its first team-building exercise: what's your name, where are you from, and what's the most embarrassing nickname that you've ever had? So, after everybody watched me wheel in late, my turn came, and I said, "I'm Rich Donovan, I'm from Toronto, Canada. I was a risk analyst in my former life, that being three months ago, and the funniest nickname I ever had was Little Dickie." Laughter ensued. There's something very Canadian about self-deprecation. Immediately I was both funny and vulnerable. It allowed my new classmates to relax and see me as one of them—or at least that's how I am choosing to tell the story. That was a very stressful moment for me, because there was a lot wrapped up in those thirty seconds. I look back now and think that it couldn't have gone better than it did. It was the start of sixty friendships.

The Columbia campus wasn't accessible in the contemporary sense of the word, but there were ways to get around that were not necessarily obvious. Under the famous steps up to the library that you see in the movies, a tunnel with an elevator leads to the upper campus, where the business school is.

They gave me a little golden key to operate the elevator at any time of day or night—shades of Harry Potter. It made getting home interesting at times. It was a speed bump, if you will. You had to make sure that you didn't get too silly at the pub, because you had to be able to operate the elevator. If you didn't have a key, you needed a security guard to operate it for you.

By the end of my time there, after discovering and opening back doors and secret tunnels, the campus security guards knew me quite well. I figured out all the back ways through campus, including a path right by the old laboratory where the Manhattan Project originated. I figured them out by repeatedly getting lost until I found my way out. In three weeks, I had it nailed, and after that it took me about ten minutes to get to class.

As I mentioned, I am rarely late; I consider it a point of honor to be on time. Here's why: because I have a disability, people have expectations of me that are generally low. To shatter those expectations, I must excel, every time. Some of excellence is talent, but most of it is process. Most of excellence is stepping back from a deliverable to assess what is required, and doing the things you need to do to achieve the best result.

That's important when you have a disability. I do not have the luxury to take the same things for granted that many people can. If I need a gallon of milk, I can't just throw on a coat and head out. I have become fastidious with time and with process to exceed expectations. Not just to meet expectations but to exceed them: to be the best at what I do, whether it's buying a carton of milk or building an index fund. This is especially true in recent years, because, like it or not, I have a public persona and I stick out like a sore thumb in many cases. That comes with a responsibility to always at least appear to know what I'm doing.

Before I got to New York, I was scared—but in a good way. It was the kind of trepidation where you feel everything and feel very alive. I don't remember much about the first six months at Columbia, but I think it was similar to professional sports. Pro athletes get so in sync with what they are doing that they don't even think about it. I was working on muscle memory most of the time. The rigor of the process that I put into place each day really helped me: get up early, shower, eat, and plan how I was going to do the things I needed to do. I was totally out of my comfort zone. It was awesome. It was the best time of my life. The best analogy I can think of for those first six months is being shot out of a cannon. You have two choices: enjoy it, or scream and crap your pants all the way.

CHAPTER TEN

THE RECRUITING GAME

I t was the year 2000, a momentous one to start the master's program at Columbia Business School. I will admit I found the priorities a bit odd at first. They were, in order of importance, a) get a job, b) network with your classmates, c) go to class. Those may not have been the official priorities, but those are the priorities of most students who go into the MBA program at Columbia. Any top business school is the same. Before we even had our first class, we had our first recruiting event, in which the class was invited to a cocktail party to listen to the CEO of Citigroup at their then brand-new headquarters in Tribeca.

At these recruiting events, there's an executive team whose job is to work the room. Their purpose is twofold: to make the company look good, which is easy, and to find talented students that they want to hire. By this time, we're all twenty-six, twenty-seven, twenty-eight years old. I was twenty-five. You get a glass of wine or a beer in your hand, and you talk. The recruiters want to build relationships so that when students come back for interviews, the foundation is there. I was selling myself right from the get-go.

I quickly learned that if you're at Columbia, firms assume a certain level of intelligence or chutzpah. So you're already worth considering. Their challenge is finding the talents who are going to turn into future producers of value for the firm, the men and women who are going to change the business for them in ten years. I believe that 10 to 20 percent of my class is going to change the world. That's what happened with the class before that, and the class before that. It's the same with every top business school.

At that Citi recruiting event, I realized that I had a big asset; I just didn't know quite how big it was. Wherever I went, I would get a good look. I didn't need to compete for face time. I was going to get an interview just by engaging. That was good, but I was still quite stressed out, because I had to convince everyone that I could do the job. From September to March, my world revolved around convincing a bank to hire me. Added to that already complex challenge is the fact that even I wasn't sure I could physically perform the job of trader—my chosen goal.

Every day, it seemed, there was an event. Over the course of September, October, and November, I visited every major trading floor in Manhattan. I did these off-campus events on my feet. I don't know exactly how I did that, but I don't remember it being a struggle. I never asked for special anything, although I was offered the red-carpet treatment quite a bit. My job was to position myself as a trader. I was there to prove beyond the shadow of a doubt that I could do the job.

I rarely discussed disability. I talked markets, risk. Most of my colleagues were already in finance and had a banking background or a research background. I was one of two or three people with a risk background, which gave me an edge. That and the profile I got just from walking into the room put me in a very good position to sell myself.

Visiting trading floors was an interesting experience. They are vast, open spaces where there really are no secrets. Each trader needs to see what's happening on the floor, so the whole room sees who is coming and going. Whenever I walked onto a trading floor, people noticed. Nobody else looked remotely like me. People would pop up and down to look. Stand up, look, sit down. Stand up, look, sit down. I used to call it Whac-A-Mole. But because I was such an anomaly, I had serious conversations with everybody. I'm sure that I wasn't just having conversations—I was also the topic of conversation. Like, *Wait a second. What I'm seeing doesn't click with what I hear. This guy shouldn't be this intelligent. Right? This isn't what I'm used to.* I could read it on their faces. It was not wholly unexpected, either. If you had no frame of reference for disability, how could you be expected to understand it?

I was trying to play it straight and get a job. I wasn't thinking about the effect I was having. But looking back on it, now that I'm more aware of how it works, I think that must have been quite a shocker for most people. It was cool that they adapted and included me in the mix. They had to fill their numbers in diversity categories, but those categories included women and people of color. The 1990s had just finished, and disability wasn't on the radar for most employers. I was outside of what they expected.

Just because I was having serious conversations with everybody didn't mean I was going to win everyone over. I was a little bombastic back then. I thought I needed to be, and I probably did. I needed to talk about the markets like I knew exactly what I was doing. Maybe the reality was that I didn't have a clue, but I decided I wasn't going to let them see me sweat. I was twenty-five, I barely knew what I didn't know, but I prepared myself to talk intelligently about the markets and express my opinion in a confident way.

I would start off by saying that I didn't know with certainty, but then I would explore the probabilities of something happening. This is essentially the language of risk. I would be asked, "What's your take on internet stocks today?" because at the time we were going through massive revaluations of technology firms. Or I would be asked about Enron. WorldCom was going on, Tyco was happening. You needed to have an opinion. It didn't necessarily have to be right, but you needed to have an opinion that demonstrated an intelligent view of global markets, global politics, and global banking. I was talking with managing directors and their teams that lived and breathed markets daily. You had to at least sound like you belonged, like you weren't out of your league.

I learned that when auditioning for an opportunity that matters, you need to show you are confident enough to have opinions and defend them effectively. Your counterparts aren't really concerned with whether you're right about the outcomes. That's outside of your control anyway. The recruiters want to see how you perform in their environment. Your possible employer doesn't expect or even want you to really know what's happening deep inside their company. They want to see how you carry yourself, think things through, and make judgments.

Despite my determination to show confidence, a gentleman I'll call Simon Rhodes was a guy I found a bit intimidating. Simon was an executive-in-residence at the Business School. He was there to advise us on how things worked and give us his opinion on how we should position ourselves. Simon was a former managing director at an investment bank. I remember telling him, "Okay, here's what I want to do, I want to be a trader, this is my background—"

He cut me short. "All right, let's get down to brass tacks here. You'll never be a trader. You don't have the ability to yell out prices, you're not able to move fast enough. You're not able to communicate the way a trader needs to, you can't talk on the phone in the right way. You'll be a very good risk manager. Your background is what the Street needs, they're always looking for risk managers."

I didn't want to hear that. I wanted to be producing, on the revenue side, because that's where the action is. I was polite. I thanked the man. Inside, I wanted to rip his face off. I was thinking, *How dare you tell me what I can't do!* I had been meeting people like him my entire life, but almost none of them had the balls to say it. Simon did. I give him credit for that. He was wrong, but he wasn't the last person to tell me what I couldn't do.

In the Columbia recruiting world at that time, employers focused on recruiting from September to February, going through this process of initial event, invite-only event, Super Saturday, job offer. All the initial activity happens in the first three months of the first semester, and then you have Super Saturdays in January, when the banks invite in their top picks. They put candidates through a daylong process of interviews and decide whether they really want them. Each year, the final rounds of the recruiting at most banks include sixty or eighty of the best MBAs from Harvard, Wharton, Stanford, Columbia, Chicago, Carnegie Mellon—all the top business schools. It's the last step in the process before they make an offer.

I went through this process with about twelve banks. On the Monday after my last Super Saturday, I was heading to a lecture when a classmate of mine stopped me in the hallway. "Rich," he said, "can I talk to you? I'm not quite sure how to tell you this, but a good friend of mind is a recruiter at Deutsche Bank, and we were having drinks with some people the other night, and he confided in me that although you were an impressive candidate, there was no way Deutsche Bank would hire a disabled guy."

I thanked him and continued my way. That was just one guy talking, but at that point I had yet to get an offer, because it was so early in the process. I thought, *Oh my God, what if every other* *bank thinks the same way? Did I just spend $150,000 on a piece a paper and will not get a job out of it?* My parents had mortgaged their house to send me to school. It was a terrifying moment. I was crushed for about a week. But it was a very human moment too. It took a lot of guts for that guy to tell me that. I'm glad he did. It was a wake-up call for me. Up until that day, the process had been very easy for me: attend some events, interview, get a job offer. That's the way I thought it worked. But what I had just heard came from the customer's mouth. And I've always learned that anything from the customer's mouth is gospel. My mind immediately jumped to *Oh, no. Everyone else is thinking the same way. I'm the only guy who isn't.*

I was in agony for four days. I could barely eat or sleep. I realized that in two weeks I could be screwed over and embarrassed. That thought had never dawned on me before. I had never considered the possibility that I could fail. Then, after a week of torture, the offers for sales and trading internships started to come in: Merrill, Goldman, Deutsche Bank (yes, that one). I ultimately got to look at every bank on the Street, domestic and foreign. I think I interviewed at thirty-eight banks. That was my first exposure to volume interviewing—at least until I started dating.

Two of the big houses at the time were Merrill Lynch and Goldman Sachs. Goldman told me that I was their number one draft pick that year. When I got the offer, the other banks cranked up their efforts. I went to meetings, dinners . . . what it came down to was I got a phone call one day from the vice-chairman of Merrill Lynch, Steve Hammerman, number two at the firm. I went to meet with him. Walking down the hallway high up in 4 World Financial Center, it felt like I was going to meet the Wizard of Oz.

Steve greeted me and said, "Look, Rich, here's the deal. This is going to be challenging for you with a disability. I have a granddaughter with CP. I know what you're dealing with. Don't worry about it. We're going to make it work. We'll figure it out." And for me, that was it.

But I wouldn't be much of a salesman if I had left it there. I wanted to take it to Goldman. I wouldn't call it shopping, but I wanted to give them a chance to respond before I said no. In choosing Merrill, I had the opportunity to manage my risk with senior-level support. This decision was a difficult one to make, but the kind of decision that made the effort to get there well worth it.

I was faced with uncertainty about a career that I didn't even know I could manage. I traded to reduce my risk. I figured if I had the vice-chairman of the firm telling me that he had my back, that was valuable insurance. I didn't know how this was going to play out. I knew I could do the job, but there was a lot of uncertainty. I barely understood how the business worked, let alone the politics involved or my role in it. I made the conscious decision to say, *Okay, I'm going to go where I know I'm going to get a very deep, very good look.*

I went down to Goldman's headquarters, and they said, "How can we help you? Do you have any questions? What are you thinking?" I said, "Okay. Let me lay it out for you. I just spent an hour with the vice-chairman of Merrill Lynch. He basically said, 'Don't worry. We've got your back.' If you were in my shoes, what would you do?" The guy I was talking to didn't hesitate a second. He said, "I would go to Merrill Lynch. That's unbelievable. You don't get that ever. Take it. Take it." So I did.

Little did I know there was a battle going on at the top of Merrill between the old and the new guard. The vice-chairman was part of the old guard, and he was about to hand over the reins. By the time Steve left the firm, he and many others had ensured that I had the broad-based sponsorship I needed to have the opportunity to succeed. Sponsorship does not mean success, but it does help give you the opportunity to succeed or fail based on what you deliver. Frankly, the transition at the top meant that Merrill was about to take on increased risk. That was a very good thing for me, as someone who would help manage that risk in the equities business.

The Merrill effort was interesting because earlier in the recruitment process, I had been persona non grata with the Merrill U.S. team. I mistakenly sent them an email intended for Goldman Sachs. One part of the recruiting process involved sending prompt thank-you notes to the people that you met each day. Because I don't type particularly fast, I would copy and paste eight or ten messages, changing the salutation and adding in a personal note about the individual that I met with. I still do that today, just to keep things efficient. Of the five hundred or so emails I sent in those four weeks, I slipped up on one that I sent to Merrill. The guy with whom I interviewed, whose name I can't remember now, called me out on it and essentially said, "Don't bother coming back." One slip-up, and I was blackballed from one of the top investment banks. Now, that was perfectly okay. I might have done the same. My mistake could be taken as a lack of attention to detail. I wrote the guy back, explained and excused myself, and that was that.

Then I met a Merrill executive who was recruiting for the office in London, Gary Hayes. How do I describe Gary? He is one of the kindest and most straightforward men that I have ever met. I was exploring going to London as part of my internship—because why not?—so I applied to Merrill London and got an interview. They were doing their interviewing in this big suite at the New York Waldorf, and Gary and I hit it off. He was just a prince of a man—still is. He epitomized relationship-building. Gary was running the equity trading desk in London. A Brit. I remember him saying at one point, "You're coming to Merrill." I said, "Oh really?" and he said, "Yeah. I'm going to make it my life's work to get you to Merrill. Whatever it takes."

There may be one additional reason I impressed Gary. He had to change his suite at the Waldorf at the last minute and couldn't contact all the New York interviewees ahead of time with his location. I was the only candidate to find his last-minute new suite and arrive on time for the interview. He would tell Jenn and I that story seventeen years later, over champagne in the bar at the Goring Hotel in London.

Gary and the Merrill UK team flew me over with a couple of my Columbia colleagues on a Thursday night and put us up at the Sanderson Hotel, a swanky place in central London. I spent the day at the office on Friday and put on a hard hat to do a tour of the new HQ Merrill was building in the City next to St. Paul's Cathedral. There were thirty of us, some from the U.S., some from the U.K., and they were trying to convince us to join the team. I'm sure we all had multiple offers at the time. We finished with a big dinner at one of the local hot spots. It was great. I sat with the CEO of Merrill France, the head of the London equities team, Gary, and some other people.

Here's the funny part. I got back to my hotel and sitting on my pillow was a $300 Montblanc pen as a "sales gift." I just roared with laughter. Here they are, giving a fine piece of writing equipment to a guy who can't write. It was classic. You just can't write this stuff, pun intended. I kept that pen on my trading desk for years.

Once I got back to New York, Gary eventually said, "Look, we want to do what's best for your career. This was originally going to be a London offer, but we're making this a global offer. You can go to London, you can go to Hong Kong, you can go to Tokyo, you can go to New York or anywhere else. Take a week, think about it, and come back to us."

Now that was a great offer, but part of it was a test to see if I was serious. If I were to pick a place like Paris or Moscow, they would have an idea about where I was coming from. Those are beautiful places, but from a business perspective not so smart, especially if you're just starting on building a career. The only right choice was New York.

CHAPTER ELEVEN
MY GOLDEN KEY

Once I had chosen to go with Merrill Lynch in March of 2001, fifteen months before graduation, I was able to concentrate on the other two main activities at Columbia: networking and classes. Most people at business schools are already familiar with the material; the MBA takes it to a deeper level. I was confident that I wouldn't have a problem with the academics, but I wanted to make sure that testing didn't drag me down. After the experience I'd had at York, I decided to take a different approach at Columbia.

The first day of school, I went to see the people at the dean of students' office and said, "Okay, here's the deal. I learned a lot about myself in undergrad. I've learned what works and what doesn't work for me. I would rather be proactive with you today and get around that now, as opposed to coming back to you in six months in frustration." The administrator on the other side of the counter said, "Whatever you need, you've got it."

Once I had explained more fully, she said, "I'll speak with your profs, then you can meet with them. You can have all of your exams with your profs, anything you need to get across to them you can do it orally, we will go out of our way to make sure that you are able to communicate your knowledge."

Awesome. *Awesome*. I'm telling you, Columbia for me . . . there's a reason why I still walk around wearing a Columbia T-shirt. Honestly. I love the place. In every feasible way, it was a phenomenal experience. It was the kind of thing that I didn't expect going in, but I was blown away when it happened.

I can remember sitting with my professors. Most of them said roughly the same thing: "I'll sit with you for forty minutes and we'll have a chat, then I'll test you on your knowledge, then we'll have a take-home exam. Come back to me in three or four hours with it finished, I'll grade it, I'll assess your knowledge, and that will be your grade." That worked well. My profs could test me on my ability to analyze the material, then I would go home and build a spreadsheet or whatever technical aspect was associated with the class. It was seamless.

This workaround allowed me to focus, as my classmates were, on recruiting. That's why we all were there—to get jobs. Columbia produced an interesting analysis of Business School graduates' employment that illustrates how globalization and finance have reordered the economy—and changed the incentives for the "best and brightest." In a report on recruiting trends, the school compared the composition of employers of graduates in 1966 and fifty years later in 2016.

In 1966, more than one-third of the graduates went to work in manufacturing and another 13 percent in the energy sector. By 2016, over two-thirds of graduates went to work in either financial services (37 percent) or management consulting (35 percent). In 1966, only 3 percent of graduates were international students; fifty years later, four in ten graduates were from outside the United States.

About 70 percent of my class went to Wall Street or consulting—those were the two big streams. In 2016, you see a little more media and technology.

Wherever graduates go to work, it's likely they will be relying on what the school taught them about asset valuation and cash flow. Cash flow drives valuation, so every element of business is examined from that perspective. The magic phrase at Columbia Business School is "cash flow." And that's really the biggest takeaway for me academically: the whole mindset of thinking of cash flow as the lifeblood of a business. It's not about profit and loss, because you can always flash short-term profit by cutting cost. Cash flow is what keeps a business going and growing.

In my own business, cash flow is king. Even though I have global clients, mine is still a small business. Pay vendors, pay employees, build content, eat, invest . . . all of that takes cash flow. Columbia wasn't academically rigorous for me because I already knew the basic material, but the focus on cash flow greatly influences the way I operate, first as a trader and then as a business owner. Cash flow is joined at the hip to risk. As I first learned at OFA, if you can measure risk, you can measure price. When a good or service or financial instrument takes on greater risk, the purchaser pays a lower price. People don't like uncertainty, and risk is a measure of uncertainty. So the price of a good or service or financial instrument incorporates all its various risks. Highly trusted and reliable brands earn their premium in the marketplace because of their historic consistency.

In the bond market, if the government of Canada promises to pay you $1 million, the likelihood of getting paid is pretty good. If it's the government of North Korea, your risk of not getting paid is higher. So the cash flow from Canada is worth more than the cash flow from North Korea. That's how risk and cash flow work together. And that's the essence of business. The ability to develop and trade ideas for cash is entrepreneurship. The ability to understand the likelihood of that cash landing in your bank account is risk management. I had the risk-management piece; I didn't have the cash flow piece. Columbia helped me to understand how that works. It sounds simple, but it's not. If you figure out how to make it work in every facet of business, you're a multibillionaire.

For a trader, that knowledge is invaluable. If the U.S. dollar takes a dive, it influences certain companies in terms of cash flow. If you are Caterpillar, suddenly it becomes a whole lot more attractive to sell abroad. If you have 50 percent of your cash flow outside the U.S. and the dollar takes a 10 percent dip, that cash flow is now worth $550 million rather than $500 million, simplistically speaking. Nothing else has changed, but that cash flow has just gone up. On the other side of the coin, if you are Walmart and you import most of your goods from China, it's not so good. As a trader in that state of the world, I'm going to buy Caterpillar and sell Walmart.

Columbia's influential work in cash flow became more critical after the 2007–08 financial crash. As noted in *A Century of Ideas*, a history of the Business School edited by Brian Thomas and published in 2016, Professor Patrick Bolton plowed important new ground in cash flow dynamics:

> For firms under pressure cash in hand can be worth more than its face value. If the firm has cash, it can continue to operate, boosting its chances of survival during a rough patch. When the money runs dry, however, firms may find they cannot raise more cash and will have to fold; or, less drastically, they may find that they can raise cash only on onerous

terms. For this reason, the size of the firm's cash holdings affects all other corporate decisions, especially in a crisis.

To explore cash valuation, Bolton and his colleague Neng Wang built a quantitative dynamic model representing a simplified firm to estimate the actual value of the marginal dollar. When a firm runs low on cash, they found, an actual dollar can be worth as much as five times its face value.

These are the kinds of lessons you learn at Columbia. They go way beyond textbooks. I loved the class on leadership I took with Professor Mike Feiner, a master at making material come to life. He spent his career leading HR at PepsiCo. Mike had a way of making things uncomplicated. He would say things like "Your career is very simple. It hinges on one four-letter word: 'ship.'" Always be shipping. Always be delivering something that someone wants. Whether that is internally with your boss, whether that is externally with customers, your reputation and your career depend on your ability to ship. That's the practical kind of thing that you don't learn in a typical textbook.

He explained that each of us sets limits on his or her own success. If you want to go to your kid's baseball game, for example, leave the office and go to your kid's baseball game. These are things that young, hungry, inexperienced MBAs tend not to think about.

Mike highlighted the soft skills. You can do all the financial modeling, all the hard-core numbers and calculus and all that good stuff, but at the end of the day business is about relationships. You've got to work at those. These were valuable lessons to me as an MBA student—I wasn't going to learn them anywhere else. A year later, in my career at Merrill, I used them every day. I still use them every day. Life lessons like build relationships and be candid with people; don't pussyfoot around. If you have unwelcome news to deliver, deliver it. Honestly. That's valuable, especially in large corporations. Still, soft skills can't be your product. That was always Mike's point. At the end of the day you still have to ship, to deliver value to somebody. If you build a culture of shippers, your people are more likely to be productive and happy.

I love how Mike taught that class, and we stayed in touch. As I was finishing this book, I happened to hear from him about connecting with a colleague of his. Whenever I have the chance, I pass on Mike's wisdom. The least I can do is pay it forward. By the way, I also love his book, *The Feiner Points of Leadership*. It's well worth your time and ten bucks.

Another valuable course that I took in my second year was Negotiations. It was phenomenal, especially for a trader. Professor Seth Freeman taught us how to structure negotiations. How to set offers, how to set bids, how to move off offers and toward bids, and to know when to walk away, which is *the* most important thing to be able to do in a negotiation. It's called BATNA, short for "best alternative to no agreement." That has always stuck with me. Basically, if you walk away—that being the nuclear option—is it better than doing something else? So when you're going into a negotiation, it's important to already know the absolute minimum you will accept before you walk away. Know it and be ready to use all your tools at any time to your advantage.

Another crucial thing that course taught me was that you have no idea what your opponent wants. Your opponent's BATNA might be above your top ask. Your top ask could be an amazing deal for the other side, in which case it's too low. When you negotiate, the other party may have a completely different value structure from yours. Even if you think you know your opponent, assume you don't.

The first rule of negotiations is: don't speak first. Because that sets the anchor. So you prolong things, you chat, you wait for them to start. That's part of the game. I want as much information as I can get before I even open my mouth. I want to know everything I can. I may have huge size behind, as they say in the industry. I've had billions of dollars in trades to do and started negotiations with $50 million to see where it's going to go, to see where I can move. A two-penny spread on a billion dollars is a lot of money, so you never show your hand. It's very much like poker. So, I'm going to test the market with $50 million and see what market I can get.

But if you have $10 billion to sell and the other side knows it, they are going to drive the price down as low as they can. You do what you can to make that bid come up. You're not going to put a billion dollars in the offer. You do a million here, a million there . . . a thousand trades of $1 million, all day long. But every second that you hold it, you're taking a risk that the price will drop. As a trader, that course in negotiations helped me define my process, a process that was repeatable and teachable and scalable. I loved that course.

As I said earlier, Columbia Business School is perhaps best known for its value investing courses. I took one with Professor Joel Greenblatt called Securities Analysis that taught me hardcore valuation techniques, those that apply to longer-term buy-and-hold investing. One year, two years, five years, sixteen years—eighty years. That's the way a lot of people invest for retirement, and it's pretty much the opposite of how we traded. In trading, a week was a long time. As a trader, I was looking more at pricing dislocation—what something should be worth in a couple of days versus a couple of years. I'm trying to realize returns from those price dislocations in a day, in a week, in two weeks. A trader is looking for a deal to happen quickly to reset the value of assets. As a trader at Merrill, I had been known to hold positions for months, but my desk's average hold-to-sell period would probably have been two weeks. In my current role as an investor, I've gone back to the twenty- to eighty-year horizon.

I underplay the academic part of Columbia, but it was busy. We probably had two or three group projects due every week. We would spend most of our time at the library, which is a different place at a business school than it is elsewhere. It's not full of books and people going "shhh!" It's full of tables with groups around them talking about various assignments. And you had people going from group to group, saying, "How did you figure this project out? What are you doing for this project?" It was very collaborative. Whether it was a case study or a model that you were building, you would never go back to your room and study with your blinders on. Everything was teamwork. I would say that about 60 percent of the networking I did was directly tied to classwork. You were spending time with your teams, day in, day out, figuring out problems, doing cases together. And being good students, it wasn't like we put in an hour a day, gradually completing assignments. It was generally like, "Yikes, it's due tomorrow, we'll meet at four o'clock and work until it's done." When you did that five times a week, you got to know each other pretty well. I was usually the only quant in my group, so people relied on me for certain kinds of knowledge. "Quant" means "quantitatively oriented," though I'm not a true quant. A true quant is someone with a Ph.D. in mathematics. If you're a true quant, I can put you in a room and tell you to figure out how to get us to the moon. When I come back in three hours, you can tell me how it's going to work. That's a true quant. I can't do that.

There are generally three types of people in investment houses: quant, trader, banker. Bankers are not math whizzes, but they're great at relationships. Traders are decent at math and they're okay at relationships. Quants are human calculators, but there's a reason why most aren't client-facing. Most risk managers are quants. I'm a poser quant—the guy who sits in between the real quants and the non-quants. I can talk both languages, but you don't want me flying the plane. I guess I was a quant trader. It was the ideal situation because I could move between both worlds. Even though the quants didn't give me the respect that I would get as a quant, they knew I could keep up. I wasn't a knuckle dragger. And the traders gave me the respect due to a true quant even if I didn't deserve it. I could speak the language and do some of what a quant does even though I didn't have a Ph.D. in mathematics.

Today, quantitative analysis plays a bigger role in trading and portfolio management than ever. Trillions of dollars of capital are moved through markets based on the algorithms traders bake into their software. Computerized trade transactions occur in nanoseconds, and that's going to beat a human every time. The weakness of these algorithms tends to be portfolio risk management, as often they miss risks that they are not intentionally targeting.

Investing over the long term requires nuances of approach and strategy that few algorithms can provide—yet. A baseball player is not the sum of his sabermetric statistics and neither is a portfolio solely a reflection of algorithmic engineering. Quants tend to forget that stuff works until it doesn't work. A hero of mine, the trader and author Nassim Taleb, has demolished the rule that quantitative analysis provides a scientific shelter against the randomness of events, human frailty, and all our various cognitive biases.

I love what Taleb wrote in *The Black Swan*:

> Can we judge the success of people by their raw performance and personal wealth? Sometimes—but not always. We will see how, at any point in time, a large section of businessmen with outstanding track records will be no better than randomly thrown darts. More curiously, and owing to a peculiar bias, cases will abound of the least-skilled businessmen being the richest. However, they will fail to account for the role of luck in their performance. Lucky

fools do not bear the slightest suspicion that they may be lucky fools—by definition, they do not know they belong in such a category.

One of the hallmarks of Columbia is that they tend not to graduate lucky fools. Every signal is about developing rigorously trained, keenly sharpened financial and business judgment. The people who make it to the Business School come from all over the world with a variety of strengths and skills. They will say that the school's approach brought out their best and forced them to confront the biases in their thinking.

My classmates were everything from actors to Olympians to Marines to nuclear negotiators. Because of our divergent backgrounds and viewpoints, the conversations both in class and at the bar were phenomenal. Just rich with content. And all this is taking place in Manhattan, at events hosted at landmarks, whether they be restaurants, bars, museums, public spaces, offices, or even a hunk of urban greenery. It's the kind of experience that you just can't buy. It's hard to explain how it changes your viewpoint of the world. Because it's so immersive, for the first six to eight months you just go. You don't reflect, you just go with it, and then it becomes second nature. You're forced to step your game up by default. If you don't keep up and you don't change your thinking when you do things, a) you miss value, b) you miss out on relationships, and c) you're not maximizing your experience at the Business School. In hindsight, I should have done more looking around and saying, *Wow I'm actually doing this.* But I was just too busy doing, just trying to keep up, trying to keep pace.

CHAPTER TWELVE
FLY ME TO THE MOON

The first social event I recall was in the first semester. The Fall Ball was hosted in the ballroom of the New York Public Library, an iconic building on Fifth Avenue. Why a public library has a ballroom I'll never know, but this one did. The place was gorgeous. So here I am, this wide-eyed twenty-five-year-old Canadian kid, walking into this event, with everyone decked out in their finest. I think I was wearing a tie; most men were wearing tuxedos. I hadn't quite gotten there yet. But I remember walking in, with the orchestra playing "Fly Me to the Moon," and for the first time in the months after arriving I thought, *Okay, I'm here, I've arrived. Let's do this.*

That was the first reflective moment that I remember. Reflection is important because it grounds me and either teaches me what I screwed up or confirms that I'm doing the right thing. At that point, I felt comfortable that I was in the right space, doing what I was supposed to and not in way over my head. I stopped treading water and started to swim. I knew people, and we had been starting to develop relationships. I was still a little bit . . . I wouldn't say socially awkward, but I had never been a big-room guy. Big rooms are not ideal for me. Because of my voice and the way I walk, it's hard to navigate large rooms and be heard in large crowds. So I found a seat and started a conversation. I remember that at that point the room came to me; people would come by and chat as they circulated.

Then Bob came by and told me to get off my ass. Bob Ball was one of the student leaders at the time. He was a year ahead of us and was helping to run the various social events at the school. He was always a bit of an instigator, so he swaggered over, saying, "Get off your ass, Rich, let's go dance," probably thinking I would say no and clearly surprised when I got up. Dancing with my colleagues became a bit of a show. Because here I was, this guy who was pretty buttoned up, pretty aggressive on the recruiting side— by then I think I had solidified my reputation as at least passingly intelligent—so I think this was a little bit of a wake-up call that said, "Hey, I can party hard too."

We did a lot of that from then on. There were many separate occasions. Tuesday was an occasion. Thursday was an occasion. It helped cement relationships. We were going out, night after night, attending every social event, mingling, being gregarious, which for me was . . . I wouldn't say different, but it wasn't something I had mastered.

I was coming out of my shell and gaining incredible amounts of confidence, competing at a whole new level. That allowed me to let my defenses down and just be myself, throw caution to the wind and not think of doing things in terms of risk but in terms of having fun. Having a good time. I could do that because we were all in the same boat. Very few students at Columbia were native New Yorkers. They came from Kansas, California, Greece, Japan,

Canada, Argentina . . . we had people from all over the world at Columbia, and we all had to bond.

My reaction to Bob was a good example of how I was changing. My muscle memory was to sit down. At Columbia, guys like Bob reached out to make sure I didn't do that. It changed my muscle memory. I would find a place where I could be in the middle of things, like perched on a barstool rather than tucked into a corner table. That was a substantial change. I never wore jeans until business school, because I thought they were too rebellious. I would focus on doing things perfectly. It wasn't until I started to get comfortable with the idea that "Hey, you can actually enjoy yourself while you're doing this" that I took the stick out of my ass. A lot of it was simply understanding that people were eager to make me part of the equation. It allowed me to relax—if you're always worried about falling on your ass, you're never going to take a step forward.

The anchor night for going out was Thursdays. That was pub night, so after class you would go out with your colleagues and professors and have a couple on campus, often at a social event put on by the student council in the cafeteria. They would tap a couple of kegs. Some weeks there would be a live band, some weeks a DJ. You would do the typical theme things—costumes and decorations and all that good stuff.

After pub night, we would go to Indigo, a bar on the Upper West Side at Eighty-Third and Amsterdam, mainly because the owners were receptive. They knew that if they got two hundred Columbia MBAs into the bar for a few hours, they would make some money. It was interesting for me, because I'm not exactly the most stable guy on my feet. By the time we got to Indigo, everyone would have had a few, and the place would be packed. Indigo was my training ground for learning how to navigate big crowds, tight rooms, and tight spaces. I got to be pretty good at working my way through a crowded bar without falling down.

And of course, the big joke—half joke, half true—was "Rich walks straighter after a few drinks." A lot of CP's spasticity is caused by muscles being tight all the time. As the spasticity relaxes, I speed up. I do find it easier to walk after two or three drinks, but of course there's a point where it goes the other way and you get sloppy. Let's call it diminishing marginal returns. I'm not exactly a big guy, so I had to watch my intake and not hit that point too quickly. But I can't remember ever having trouble getting home—alive.

One evening (or early morning), Chip Cunningham, another instigator and now a successful entrepreneur, walked out of the Raccoon Lodge on the Upper West Side to get a cab after we closed the place down. The bunch of us that followed were happy but by no means out of control. Because of my wobble, the cabbie thought I was drunk and refused to take us. And Chip says, "No, he's not drunk, he's got CP!" Of course, the cabbie had a tough time understanding what they hell he was talking about. At that hour, cabbies didn't want to pick up a falling-down drunk because of the likelihood of messing up their cab.

All this stuff was so much fun for me because I was keeping up with these guys. They molded what they did around the reality of my disability. It never really changed what we got up to.

One story I like to tell is about Bob Ball and his Marine colleagues. Bob was an active-duty United States Marine before business school, and one night we went out with his old crew. We were in the bar and of course one of the things guys in their twenties do at a bar is drink shots. Bob, as he always does, was pushing things, egging us on to do shots of tequila. Now, I always drink through a straw. That's what works for me. I said, "Okay, I'll do a shot if you guys do it my way." So here we are in a Manhattan bar, busy as all hell, and there are twelve or fifteen people around, five of them big, burly Marines. I kind of knew I had them, because when I do a shot, I put the straw way in the back of my mouth and whatever I'm drinking goes right down the hatch. I barely taste it that way. These guys were going to put the straws on their lips, and I was guessing that they wouldn't be able to stand drinking tequila like that. I finished the shot in one go. Five U.S. Marines did not.

It was a good trick, one I would repeat when I got to Wall Street. By eleven thirty or twelve, everyone would always be sufficiently lubricated to go for it, and I found that if I could get a few people to put ten bucks on the outcome, it was an easy way to make cab fare home. Not that hanging out in bars is all I did outside of class. I joined the Columbia Sales and Training Club and the Sailing Club, and I coached the Men's Ice Hockey Club. Through clubs, I was not only doing what I enjoyed and taking advantage of what New York City had to offer but also meeting more people and building more relationships. There were probably about twenty of us who coalesced together as quick friends, and we would go out and do what twenty-five-year-olds did: enjoy ourselves.

When I joined the Sailing Club in my first year, one of the things we did was the annual Columbia Regatta. We took about forty people down to Sint Maarten, chartered half a dozen sailboats and sailed for a week. I skippered one of the boats. I had been sailing for years, so I knew what I was doing, but I had never actually taken legal control of a boat. That was a big deal for me, because I was skippering a forty-foot catamaran, sailing in blue water between Sint Maarten and St. Barths. We started out in this tiny little cove on the west coast of Sint Maarten called Oyster Bay. You would go around the island and stop into these bays and enjoy yourself, go out to eat, have a party, and then come back on the boat. As skipper, I had to remain somewhat lucid, so I wasn't partaking too much—which is a good thing, because when we rounded the northwest corner of Sint Maarten, we discovered what blue water sailing was all about. That's where open water hit shallow water and the waves got bigger. I remember sitting at the helm, five or six boats in a row, sailing around the corner and looking back at the waves. I was six feet above the water on the deck and six feet above the deck at the helm, and the waves were still well above my shoulders. We had to be in, what, twenty-five, thirty-foot swells, and I'm sitting there going, *Holy smokes, this is serious*. But it wasn't, it was entirely safe—just a new experience for me.

CHAPTER THIRTEEN
MOTHER MERRILL

My internship with Merrill Lynch started in June 2001, soon after classes ended. It was a relatively quiet time in the United States. President George W. Bush was a few months into his first term. The Fed was cutting interest rates, and the markets were humming along nicely. It was three months before the 9/11 attacks. The economy was still digesting the massive jobs growth of the tech boom and the Y2K crisis, which wasn't a crisis after all but forced everybody to upgrade their networks.

About 110 of us Merrill interns in the Global Markets group were flown into New York from all over the world for training. I was amazed by the caliber of the recruits. I was sitting with former Navy SEALs that had gone to top business schools, NASA rocket scientists, Army Rangers who had Ph.D.s in mathematics. I also appreciated that I wasn't the only Canadian at Merrill. Two sales and trading employees, Mark Slackmon and James Boyle, had also gone to Columbia. I was reassured knowing that there were guys who had come from Canada, gone to Columbia, and become successful at what they did. James was running the S&P book for options and futures, which was exactly what I wanted to do. I wanted to be an index derivatives trader. Mark was in sales, so he covered some of the biggest institutional clients on the derivatives side.

They were part of the Columbia recruiting team, and thus we spent lots of time together during that internship. I wouldn't be surprised if there was something going on behind the scenes that I had no idea about. They were probably told to look out for me. The top banks saw finding and fostering great employees as the *only* way to succeed. Merrill took recruiting very seriously. Every year, Merrill ushered new recruits through the process. They'd join the firm, rise up through the chain, and hopefully raise Merrill's game. It was critical to the business to get it right.

At first, we did a couple weeks of warm-up: classes, simulations, baseball games, and other events. About thirty of us interns were in U.S. sales and trading, both on the debt and equity sides. We saw each other every day, we did team-building exercises, and we were assigned a project to present to senior managers at the end of the summer. Merrill hosted weekly events that included having dinner with classmates, playing golf, going sailing, taking boat cruises in the harbor. All this seemed normal by then because I had been doing these kinds of events all year long. I thought it was normal to go to fancy bars and restaurants. It's what we did. That was the lifestyle.

Early on, each of us indicated interest in a "desk." They're called desks because you sit at the same four-hundred-foot-long desk with your teammates and try and build your business together. Desks were generally grouped by product type: equity derivatives, convertible bonds, portfolio trading, cash trading (stocks), foreign exchange derivatives, and fixed income derivatives—to name a few. Then the desk would choose the interns that they were interested in. Usually when you do an internship, you receive a full-time offer at the end of the summer if you do a respectable job. That can impact the next ten years of your life.

I did two rotations with equity derivatives, because that's the desk I wanted to join. I was fascinated with derivatives. I did a two-week rotation with fixed income derivatives, which was the exotics team, the hottest desk at Merrill at the time. It was run by a man named Barry Wittlin. The desk was rumored to be making significant profits for Merrill at the time.

I worked two weeks with international equities and another block with equity capital markets. For the final two weeks, I went back to where I wanted to be to finalize the deal: the portfolio trading desk, where I got hired as a trader at Merrill in 2002. I was shadowing a young trader who was maybe twenty-seven or twenty-eight. We were sitting together for a couple of days and built up a pretty good rapport. When you're an intern, they bring you a folding chair and you squeeze in between two people, watching and listening, kibitzing all day, observing what they do. They're testing you, throwing stuff at you, seeing how you deal with it.

When the markets closed at the end of the second day, the portfolio trader stood up and looked at me with a blank expression. "Look, Rich," he said, "I want to be straight with you. Don't focus on trading. You're never going to get there. You can't move fast enough, you won't be able to call out the orders." Just like Simon Rhodes! When you have a visible disability, you learn to control your reactions to the things people say. I was magnanimous and polite and told him I appreciated the advice.

By this point, I knew I could do the job. I'd had some trepidation because I had never done the job before—but the internship had solidified my confidence. I had spent three months on the various trading floors at Merrill, I had seen what traders did, and there was no doubt in my mind that I could do it. *I can do this*, I was thinking. *This is a piece of cake.*

Months later, that trader who had advised against trading was fired, along with the whole portfolio trading team. Merrill was about to bring in a new team to reinvent the approach the entire firm took to trading. Little did I know, I would be right in the middle of that revolution.

One story from that summer resonates particularly strongly for me, because it tells you about the culture at Merrill Lynch at the time. In early August, I had gone to a friend's wedding in midtown Manhattan. By that time, my habit was to spend most of my time on the dance floor. I probably should have sat down at some point, but I kept dancing and ended up falling backwards, tearing a ligament in my ankle. This happened on a Saturday night, and I was going to be at work on Monday. I called my boss, Charlie Sweeney, on Sunday morning. He was running the NASDAQ desk at that point and leading the summer intern program. An amazing guy. I would go to war for Charlie. He commiserated but I made it clear that I was coming to work on Monday. At that time, I was taking the subway downtown each day, from my Columbia apartment on the Upper West Side of Manhattan to the World Financial Center—a trip of about eight miles.

Since I couldn't walk, I decided to drive my scooter downtown, leaving around 6:45 a.m. I made it into work around eight, which was late. They were waiting for me at the front door with a wheelchair. I gingerly transferred from my scooter to the wheelchair, and we took the elevator to the fifth floor. When we got to the trading floor, Merrill had installed all these brand-new wooden ramps. Overnight they had put in seven or eight of them into and out of the trading floor, which was built like a pit, so that I could get to my desk. Wow. That should have told me a lot about the company, but I was too stubborn to think about it. I should have been in awe of what they had done, but I was too focused on getting the work done. I was thinking, *Okay, let's get to work!*

Thinking about it now, that was a pretty amazing thing to do. If I had realized that, it would have taken away a lot of stress. I should have accepted that these guys were in my corner. I had so many supporters at Merrill. Folks went out of their way to help me. It's hard to articulate what that was like. A fly on the wall would have witnessed me doing something that nobody thought possible. Through most eyes, a guy with CP, as a trader, managing billions of dollars really should not be possible.

During that time in the financial industry, a person with significant physical disabilities in a front-line revenue-generating position was virtually unheard of. Anyone in my position had so many factors working against them—physical barriers, communication barriers, expectation barriers. At Merrill before I arrived, only a handful of well-meaning parents of kids with disabilities had given a second's thought to even the simplest matters of accessibility, such as telephones and computers. I didn't care; I only wanted to be judged on my merits.

Of course, it wasn't just Merrill that had to see my situation differently; so did I. Any individual with disabilities who wants to break into a highly competitive profession at a prominent level needs to make major sacrifices in the arena to compete. You can't just be as good as everyone else; you show ways that you are better. My colleagues at Merrill were motivated to see me succeed because I had proven myself a potential asset. That's why optimizing the hiring and recruiting process to include qualified people with disabilities must be aligned with sound business decisions. It is a simple path to take the risk of doing something different when the potential rewards are both clear and likely.

This doesn't diminish my gratitude to all the people along the way who believed in my ability, including Henry Mulholland, the head of cash trading; Jarrod Yuster; Mike Stewart; Michael Lynch;

and Tom Patrick. All the senior managers of the trading floor were big supporters. It wasn't something that I was constantly aware of. It wasn't like there was a cheering section off to one side, but the support was real. Still, I had to produce a positive result. I don't care who you are, you don't get to do billion-dollar trades if you are without talent and motivation. Now, I don't take victory laps, because that's not the kind of guy I am, and I also don't take the time to stop to shake the hands of people who are supporting me constantly, either. Frankly I don't like being helped. I appreciate it, but I can't say I like it, if that makes any sense. These guys probably did exactly what my dad did. They probably said to themselves, *Okay, let's see what this guy can do.* And allowed me my little failures along the way, like all the other rookies.

CHAPTER FOURTEEN
9/11 AND A NEW PATH FORWARD

T he morning of September 11, 2001, I was getting ready for class in my apartment at the corner of West 119th Street and Morningside Drive. My second year at Columbia Business School had just started. I remember I had gotten out of the shower and was watching CNBC, as I did every morning to catch up on the business news. A few minutes after the first plane hit the North Tower, at eight forty-five, the reporting switched to full-on World Trade Center. Soon the entire world saw the second jet hit the South Tower; both buildings were on fire. Along with everyone else at that moment, I realized New York was under attack. Despite being glued to the television, I remember saying to myself, *I need to get out of the apartment, I need to get to the Business School*. I wanted to be around people.

Columbia canceled classes that day, obviously, because a lot of us knew people—alumni, relatives, what have you—either in the immediate area or in the towers themselves. It was a day of difficult emotions, of terror and tragedy, fear for the immediate and near future. I clearly remember sitting in my apartment that night, up on a cliff overlooking East Harlem and the Harlem River, thinking, *What's next? What's coming after this? Am I going to see a flash?*

I will never forget people walking north from downtown. By eleven in the morning, they got as far as Columbia. You could see streams of people walking up Amsterdam and Broadway to get home, covered in dust. I will never forget the sights and smells of that. It was a horrible day but also a very human day. Up until then, life for me was tightly scripted, where I did this and this happened; I did that and that happened. What I began to realize that day is that there are things in the world that are not quite so simple. Not everything is daffodils and brown sugar and white picket fences. It's not about theory and it's not about a distant land that you see on TV. There's a lot of dirty in the world. There's a battle going on for all manner of things that you don't control and that will demand you pay attention. These exogenous events need to be part of the equation. Whether they're eliminated or changed, it's not just an antiseptic march to the brass ring. Things get dirty. And that's okay. I think that's what it taught me: you must be ready for the dirty as much as for the clean.

My classmates and I were no different. We were mostly foreigners in a big city that was dealt a trauma that hung over the streets, an anxious fog. There was no dust and debris where we were, but there was a smell, like an electrical fire, that lingered for weeks. I was all the way uptown, nowhere near the event, but the Merrill office was right across the street at 4 World Financial Center. I had accepted a full-time offer on September 10, and my friends and I had gone out to celebrate with a few pops. I was supposed to go down there on the morning of the 11th to shake hands and kiss babies, so to speak. I would have been fine, but I would have been caught up in the chaos.

I had a unique take on the whole thing for one main reason: I don't cook. I had to go out to eat a lot. I would either get takeout or meet people in restaurants. For about three weeks, maybe even four weeks, nobody went out. Often, I would be the only guy outside other than the ubiquitous cop on every street corner. In New York City, being the only one on the street at 7 p.m. is a strange feeling. I was the only guy doing these things, because I had to. While the city retrenched, it went inside itself. Yet here are these entrepreneurs, these business owners, who had to pay the bills. Because I was the only customer, we talked, and it was fascinating to see this wound and its healing through their eyes.

September 11 is the day I became a New Yorker. When the city changes so dramatically, you go quickly from being a foreigner in a big city to a local. Watching my neighbors' businesses struggling, watching this vibrant city shut down for weeks . . . it was mind-boggling. I give the Business School tons of credit, because they kept going. For a lot of us, our classmates were our family. We were living together because that's all we had. It was important that the school keep moving forward, that classes keep going, that we refuse to be held at bay.

The Business School made concerted efforts to move events downtown. It was clear to me that's what was going on. The downtown economy was destroyed. As with many New York companies and institutions, the Business School community sought out meeting spaces, restaurants, bars, what have you, as close to ground zero as we could get, to support the local economy. I thought that was great. The school also pooled talents with other universities to offer free consulting to businesses struggling to survive the aftermath.

Some may believe that establishments like Columbia and money-center banks, these large hundreds-of-years-old institutions, are monolithic. It's easy to think they just sit there and suck up oxygen. But they drive something that's very human. You don't get to see that every day, but after 9/11 you saw it everywhere.

◢

On graduation day, I was joined by Mom and my brother, Mike. My grandmother Frances had just passed away, and Dad represented our family at her funeral—a time for reflection on her full life, and frankly a time for celebration of what was to come.

I moved off campus into an apartment at the end of May 2002. I found one three blocks south of the World Trade Center ruins, viewing it on the day that they reopened West Street, the highway that sat between the World Trade Center and the World Financial Center. Merrill was three blocks up, right across the street from the World Trade Center site. The site wasn't a hole at that time; it was still a pile, even nine months later. The Merrill team had been relocated to various other offices, and now, over half a year later, they moved back into the World Financial Center.

I chose to live in the financial district down by Battery Park because it was three blocks from the office. I had to be at work early in the morning and would probably be staying late at night, and I didn't want to commute. My apartment was awesome. It was on the twenty-fifth floor of Le Rivage, a landmark Art Deco building with high ceilings and large windows overlooking the World Trade Center and the Hudson River. I loved that place. It was perfect. They had taken this old building and gutted it, updating it with modern amenities. It was just perfect for me. I could just roll in and roll out. My scooter fit in the elevator, which was typically a challenge in New York City, the land of the small elevator. I could jump out of bed, hop in the shower, and be on the trading floor ten minutes after leaving my door. It took a lot of uncertainty out of my daily equation: the subways weren't accessible, and I didn't want to have to deal with weather impacting my ability to get cabs every day. By living so close, I controlled my commute. The scooter I had at the time could handle any weather. It blew through snow like a bulldozer. My neighborhood had bigger storms because we were on the tip of the island, right by the ocean, and we would get these nor'easters coming through. We had the odd three feet of snowfall, and I would get plastered with snow driving my scooter to work, just flying. It was great.

Manhattan was expensive, but I watched every dime. In all the ways I could, I lived like a monk. To get me here, my parents had mortgaged their house. The loan was in my name, but it was with their collateral. Man, was that stressful. I hated owing the bank who had my student loan backed by my parents' home. I felt so guilty. I'm sure they didn't care at all, but I didn't want them on the hook for money I owed, because I thought they had made a major sacrifice for me. I paid the bank back as quickly as I possibly could.

Every dime that I spent at Columbia was debt: tuition, housing, spending money, booze . . . but every time I got the opportunity to pay that down, I took it. Columbia cost me $130,000—one of the best investments I will ever make. I made $25,000 from my internship and that went into paying off debt. I took it right back out the next school year, but what the hell are you going to do? Once I graduated, any money that wasn't for rent or food was going to pay that loan. I managed to pay the bank back in my second year out of school. By my third year out of school, I was debt-free. Getting there gave me a sense of relief more than a sense of accomplishment. It had been a big burden that I wanted to be rid of as quickly as possible.

I came on full time with Merrill Lynch in June 2002. When you join an investment bank from business school, you go through a two- to three-month training program with all your colleagues. There are a few reasons for this: to bond with the firm and your classmates, to learn the ins and outs of how an investment bank works, and from a practical standpoint you must get registered with the regulatory authorities before you can do anything. You can't interact with clients, you can't touch trades, you can't make any real decisions until you have been registered with the Financial Industry Regulatory Authority, a self-policing body that regulates brokers, traders, and bankers.

The training program started at 222 Broadway. They put all the sales and trading hires and investment banking hires together in one spacious room. It was known as the Gekko Room because it was used as Gordon Gekko's office in *Wall Street*. The only resemblance to the movie set are the windows, as the space was at the time structured as a large training room. The funny thing is, Oliver Stone intended that movie to be a skew job on Wall Street. He was trying to tell people that Wall Street was a place for greedy bastards. But he unknowingly created a recruiting video for traders who were fascinated with the complexity of the financial world.

We all did the common stuff—like culture, regulations, and economics—together. Then we split into our respective groups. When the focus was trading simulations, the sales and trading hires would go into their room, and when the focus was valuation modeling, the bankers would go into their room. When a junior banker joins the firm, he or she generally does a lot of modeling work—a lot of valuation models, building decks, building presentations. When you're a junior banker, you're supporting senior relationship managers with building and maintaining *the content*. That's why junior bankers turn into good corporate executives: they get right into the details. They understand how companies get valued, what the variables are, and how that translates for investors. Most traders don't do that. Traders are more focused on understanding and managing risk—the variables that change the prices of assets.

This was all intense, because nobody was guaranteed a job. It was evident to any of us that if we screwed up our classes or didn't do well in our two or three months of training, we would be shown the door. There was also a rather binary matter of passing the regulatory exams—fail those and you are done. It wasn't time to relax. Management was screening each of us to see if we were in fact what they thought we were. (Later, when I was doing the recruiting, I saw how important this was.) We went to social events, bonded in the classroom, went out to dinners, and took groups to Yankees and Mets games—all part of our cultural indoctrination. At the time, Merrill had a strong culture. The firm was known as "Mother Merrill." If you took care of your customer, Merrill had your back.

Overall, I was comfortable about how I was doing. I'm fascinated by complex machines. The market is a complex machine. For me this was a world where I could indulge my proclivity for complexity and my natural curiosity for how things worked together—and do so in an environment where I had the opportunity to earn some money. The money was a bonus. I've never had a monetary goal. My theory was, and still is, that if you work to be the best at something, the money will follow. But you should be realistic. I don't know of many wealthy worm pickers. Suffice to say that it's wise to work at something that people want and to get paid enough to earn a good living from it.

One clue that I was going to be a successful trader was in a Merrill trading simulation. The simulation unfolded over several days, testing us in real time.

I was sitting in the middle of the room, surrounded by thirty other new hires. No coffee; I was ready to rumble. We were each given a book of stocks, some capital, and set up on a computer network linked to the instructor who ran the controlling computer. We traded against our colleagues and the instructor, who was throwing us curveballs constantly.

I went about my trading strategy. With my training in risk management, I traded my way in and out of risk. I was trading the odds for incremental returns, building up my margins carefully by taking smart and brief risks. My colleagues were largely running trades to make money; I was trying not to lose money.

When the instructor saw us doing too well, he upped the level of difficulty by adding more volatility, or surprises in the "news." I can't remember what happened numerically, but I do remember crushing the simulation. Just crushing it. Returns were high, risk was low. It was a simple model, but there were many variables that you had to manage, including positions overnight and the risks that you were taking in terms of bid/ask spreads, how you were getting rid of positions and getting stuck with positions if they were going against you . . . typical building blocks of trading. The instructor did this same simulation for all the trading houses, training people on simulators.

He came over to me afterwards and said, "You just beat my model. You're probably in the top 1 percent of all the people who have done this simulation." It meant exactly nothing because it was a simulation—it wasn't real—but it gave me the confidence to say, *Yeah, okay, I can do that.* I remember going home that day thinking, *Yup, those guys who said I couldn't do this were wrong.*

Here is the fun part—I was not using a "regular" keyboard. At the time I had two vintage 1983 King Keyboards, which are large keyboards with oversized keys about an inch in diameter. Wherever I was, those keyboards were with me. Every trade I ever made went through them. I still use them today. They don't make them anymore, so if I break them I'm screwed. I'm hoping that by the time they break, a brain-to-computer interface will be available and I won't need a keyboard anymore. It's coming. Back then, we had the Windows system and the Unix trading system on different boxes, so I needed one keyboard for each. When I joined Merrill, the firm was probably in last place of all the big investment banks from a technology perspective. That would change quickly.

By about the second month of our training program, they wanted us to start interacting with our desk. Most people had some familiarity with the teams they were joining because they had sat with them in the summer, but for me that was not the case because they had fired the entire portfolio trading team during my second year at Columbia, just after I finished my internship. Except for a few guys who didn't get sacked, I had not met anyone on the new team. And thanks to 9/11, traders weren't spending much time with the guys in the upcoming class. Things were spread in many different directions; veteran traders were worried about basic blocking and tackling because backup facilities were now primary facilities. I had kept my distance while at school because I didn't want to overstep my bounds—there were enough variables to deal with. I had never met the new team leaders, Mike Stewart and Jarrod Yuster. In orientation, the associates would go down to the floor for a couple of hours per week, sit with their new teams, and start to build relationships. I had to prove myself all over again. I had to show Mike and Jarrod that a) I knew enough to contribute to the team, and b) I could do the job. I had the added benefit of having a disability and not knowing specifically whether I could physically do it. I was open about that. I didn't hide it. I would say, "We'll find out. Game on."

I remember walking onto the trading floor in June or July, probably July, to find my new boss, Mike Stewart. When you join an investment bank or a trading team, you're not spoon-fed. It's up to you to do the things you should do for your career. It's not like somebody is going to say, "Hey, I'm going to set up a meeting with you and your new boss, so you can get to know each other and go out for coffee." You need to seek out your leaders and introduce yourself. I had never even seen Mike before. What did he look like? Today you can get on the internet and read their whole life history. Back then, that didn't exist.

I walked around the edge of the trading floor. The portfolio trading desk was located at the south end, opposite the entrance. The desk stretched on for what seemed a hundred yards. Each trader had an armchair, three screens, and assorted stationery. This was my new home. To get to portfolio trading, you have to walk through the cash pit or around past the international desk. The short way was to walk down two steps, across the cash pit and then up four steps to get to the portfolio trading desk. I always like to avoid the stairs, so I went the back way.

I tapped one of the sales guys, nicknamed Whopper, on the shoulder. "Hey, I'm looking for Mike Stewart." Whopper pointed and said, "Yeah, he's right there."

I walked up and said, "Hi, I'm Rich Donovan. Nice to meet you, Mike."

He was at his desk at the end of the row, as the desk head always was at that time. "Rich, I've heard a lot about you," he said. "Let's go have a chat."

We got along well. Mike is just a great guy. Really smart and driven, he understands how to sell and understands how to build. He has a rare combination of technical skills and selling flair. As I would learn, those were critical skills in building a new business and, at the time, very badly in demand. Merrill had virtually no portfolio trading capability in 2002.

Over the years I worked for Mike, I was consistently impressed at how he managed people. He was tasked with reinventing the equities business by leveraging data and technology. This required both building capabilities that did not currently exist and ensuring new kinds of talent were hired and empowered to build. Frankly, it also meant dismantling a legacy system that simply could not compete with data and technology. That kind of change is difficult, and it meant many of my trading colleagues would lose their jobs—the visceral price of progress. For the large part, Mike handled this well, remaining transparent and honest about the process. Later, as an entrepreneur, I would recall Mike's ability to build new businesses and his direct approach to content. My take-away from Mike was: "Build world-class content first, then sell it as your deepest passion."

CHAPTER FIFTEEN
A BIG DAY IN THE LIFE OF A TRADER

T raining gave way to working on the floor, and I quickly formed a daily routine. I wanted to be in at work by 7:00, 7:15 a.m. The first morning call was always around 7:30, 7:45, 8:00. That was when all the traders gathered in the middle of the trading floor and talked about what lay ahead for the day. We might hear from an analyst, somebody who would say, "IBM's coming out with earnings today, this is what we're expecting, this could move the markets this way, that way, the other way." A few people would chime in with updates: "Overnight we saw Japan come in and cut interest rates, this is what it did to the market, we're going to see some flow here from clients who do business in Japan . . ."

The morning call was common at the time. That was back when everything was siloed. The cash desk had their morning call, the international desk had their morning call, the derivatives desk had their morning call, the portfolio trading desk had their morning call. By my fourth year, the team I worked with had automated trading, and everything was integrated.

Mike succeeded at getting these various teams to work together; to make sure that the client got served the way the client wanted, not the way we wanted to serve them. But when I joined, each desk was discrete and protective of its prerogatives. Clients went to one desk for this, another for that, and the teams weren't really talking to each other. This was not a Merrill phenomenon; every house was structured that way.

By the time the morning meeting happened, everything was old. Only the numbers on the screen were new. I loved that about the job. Every day, every hour, was different. As the world changed, so did the market. Traders had to adapt. I may have gone into the day with a plan, but I needed to be able to change that plan on a minute-by-minute, second-by-second basis, depending on the landscape. Change came from a new player in a market, a government decision, a corporate announcement. Sometimes it took the form of a terrorist attack or a power blackout, which is what occurred a year into my career at Merrill.

On August 14, 2003, a sagging power line in Ohio brushed against some tree branches and shorted out, creating a ripple effect that sent a blackout rolling up the northeastern seaboard and into Canada. It happened around 5 p.m. the day before my first trade. Almost instantly, New York was frozen. Thousands had to be rescued from elevators stuck between floors and from subways between stations. Store owners, fearing a riot, shuttered their shops early. You couldn't get in, you couldn't get out. The trains weren't running, and pedestrians threaded their way through cars gridlocked on the Brooklyn Bridge.

It was hard for a lot of people but not for me. First, I dealt with adversity every single day. Second, I lived three blocks from Merrill. I scooted home and walked up twenty-five flights of stairs to my apartment—a challenge but one that was well lit, with five of my neighbors making the trek with me. Walking up stairs is far easier for me than walking down them. Well, the power had not yet been restored the next day, and I wasn't about to let twenty-five floors of stairs keep me from work. So, at 6:30 the next morning, I had to figure out how to get down from the twenty-fifth floor in the pitch black, with no help. The battery-powered emergency lights that had lit the way up had run out for the trip down. I had four flashlights, so the problem wasn't finding light but how to hold it and keep my hands free. I needed both hands on the railing when I went down the stairs. I decided that what I needed was a lantern that I could loop over my arm, keeping my hands free. Looking around my apartment, I saw a white plastic bag on the kitchen counter that I had used to bring groceries home. Bingo. I put the flashlight in the bag and the whole thing glowed. I put my arm through the handles and walked downstairs with this make-shift lantern swinging away on my arm, bonking my knees and clanking the metal handrail all the way down.

Merrill had backup generators, so the elevators were working, and the trading floor was fully functional—but it was a ghost town. The subways weren't running and the city was still jammed up tight, so when I walked onto the floor I was one of the only people there. Only three or four of us on the portfolio desk had been able to make it in. We needed to get to work. Out of necessity, I was going to have to trade that day. Instantly, all the trepidation and any doubts I had been harboring for more than a year went straight out the window. Sometimes you've got to prove that you want it, and for me that was the day. My first trade was an unwind of one hundred thousand shares of a lightly traded Italian furniture maker called Natuzzi. I was ready, and the trade went smoothly. I remember focusing on that trade as if I was landing a 747 on a short driveway. There was three years of preparation in that trade, and I can't even remember the profit. The dam was open. Done.

A trader's day can turn at any given moment, depending on news flow or trade flow. We had it drummed into us that you must adjust quickly and be right every single time. You can be humming along at ten thirty in the morning, thinking your day is going to look a certain way, when a client comes in with a big trade and it's all hands on deck. You do what is right for the client, you do what is right for the business, and sometimes that can mean a total about-face to a well-laid plan.

Most people hate that kind of stress, that kind of responsibility. I love it. Yes, being a little bit wrong can cost you a million dollars in the blink of an eye. But that keeps you on your toes. When you're a registered trader, you have a fiduciary duty to protect the assets of the client to the best of your ability. I've always taken my fiduciary duty extremely seriously, like the duty that I now have to my child. I see fiduciary duty as the strongest legal bond in the world. It must guide every decision you make. Mistakes still happen, but diligence can eliminate almost all mistakes.

On a trading floor, you must do several things simultaneously, all while tuning things out and tuning things in. Jenn likes to tease me about this. We will be having a conversation; I will be watching a hockey game; keeping an eye on something on the computer; talking to our son, Maverick; there will be a radio on in the background that I won't even hear; and she will be wondering if I am paying attention to what she's saying. And I'm listening to every word. I can do all that at once because of trading: traders operate amid utter chaos. Just tons of noise. You're literally shoulder-to-shoulder with your teammates. There's a guy over here getting teased by his wife on the phone about something he screwed up the night before, and you're tuning that out; there's a trader over there yelling at her teammate because she has to yell to be heard over the noise in the room, and you're tuning that out; somebody is telling a joke over here and you're tuning that out; and you're focusing on things that you need to focus on. You've got someone at your shoulder, talking at you; you're on the phone with a floor trader in Chicago; you're making a trade; and you're watching half a dozen screens. That's the job of a trader—to monitor and execute simultaneously. Especially a portfolio trader. Because you're not monitoring twelve stocks, you're monitoring thousands of stocks. And the indices. And the derivatives that go with them. So you've got lots of things going on at once, and you need to understand all of them.

In a typical day, the morning meeting lasts about fifteen minutes, then I go back to my desk and review my client orders to buy and sell. I get their trades set up for what's called the MOO: the Market on Open Order. The MOO takes all the pre-market orders and matches them with the price. So if there are more buyers than sellers, the MOO will be higher than the previous day's close, and vice versa. The number and speed of trades in the market can be bewildering if you haven't experienced it firsthand, but remember that markets are about nothing more than supply and demand. Someone is selling and wants the best price he can get; someone is buying and wants the best price she can get. Where they meet in a transaction is the price.

So I've set my orders. Then the opening bell rings, and by then everything is loaded into the computers. Your computer alerts you if something is trading off-algorithm or off-target, if there is a lot of volume, or the opposite. If there is a lot of volume in a certain stock, you typically want to speed up the trading. The system will prompt you to make decisions as you go, and you keep track of things on the screens.

Traders also support the sales team, so whatever they need to get to clients—market outlook, what you see coming, indicative pricing on risk bids, those kinds of things—you provide.

As I learned at Columbia, you never know what the seller has when you're buying, and vice versa. You may have ten million shares to sell, but she may have a hundred million shares to buy.

Your job is to find the liquidity and unwind (buy or sell) huge positions quietly. If I am selling, I need to find buyers, but I also need to sell at a fair price. If I am selling what the Street views as a lot of shares, I need to find buyers who want a lot of shares. Now if I make a big splash indicating that I have millions of shares to move, I'm like the carpet store with a going-out-of-business sale: "Liquidation sale! No offer will be turned down!" That's death to a trader on the Street. Liquidation sales have the smell of failure. So unwinding quietly is about selling without moving the price downwards. Think of it in poker terms: whether I'm holding deuce/seven or four aces, I want to go about my business at the table in a way that can't be easily read by the other players—that is, without a "tell."

Therefore, as a trader I constantly look at the trading flow for a stock and adjust. If there is a large imbalance and I've got size to move, I can put my stocks in there, there, and there. Then, once I have adjusted how and where I am willing to buy and sell the stocks, I get my index arbitrage book set up and ready to go, as well as all my baskets of stocks—the normal is four or five hundred stocks per basket—in time to put in my bid by eight forty-five to prepare for the opening print.

Most people understand the concept of stock indices, but they may have never heard of index arbitrage. It's quite simple. Arbitrage is defined by Investopedia as "the simultaneous purchase and sale of an asset to profit from a difference in the price. It is a trade that profits by exploiting the price differences of identical or very similar financial instruments on different markets or in different forms."

How does that work in the real world? If I'm running an arbitrage, I can sell, or short, a stock or group of stocks on one exchange when its future or option price, or derivative, is out of sync on another exchange. I can take a long position in cash and a short position in derivatives, or vice versa. By making these moves,

I'm protected against swings in either direction by the market. If the market moves, I lose money here and make money there. I am looking for mispricings in dividends or mispricings vis-à-vis how I expect the index makeup to change. Interest rate moves can also impact arbitrage, making yield curves a useful feast of knowledge. Arbitragers do this all day long.

Most investors don't know that arbitrage exists, nor should they care, because the price dislocations do not impact the long-term value of their investments. The mispricings last only for very short periods, gobbled up by traders that understand how these policy changes work and do the research to understand when an asset is priced wrong. Arbitrage keeps markets priced correctly. If something isn't right, arbitragers will find it, invest in it, and, in so doing, whack it back into the fair price. There's always a possibility that you're going to be wrong, but that's where due diligence comes in. On my book, we had a 97 percent hit rate. Not bad.

To do well in arbitrage, you need to be active on both sides of the market, willing to buy and sell and do things like exchange of futures for physical, or EFPs, where a stock future is exchanged for the stock itself in a single trade. This isn't buy-and-hold stuff. In arbitrage you are constantly adjusting. You can arbitrage stocks on any exchange in the world, but in the U.S. a lot of arbitrage takes place between the NYSE/NASDAQ and the Chicago Mercantile Exchange. If IBM stock is trading at one hundred dollars on the NYSE and IBM options are trading at $99.97 on the CME, you short the stock here and buy the option there. It's a solid, risk-free way of making a buck—or, more accurately, three cents. You've essentially bought and sold the same asset, at the same time, collecting a few cents on a hundred dollars. This is a (very) simplified example, but these types of dislocations are central to arbitrage and are more common than most people think.

I got to know index arbitrage very well because my first trading job was to take over the index arbitrage book. At that time, Merrill was nowhere in the arb business. My colleague Ed Cotler, now a very good friend, will tell you that nobody wanted it because that business was almost impossible, given the tools that Merrill had at that time. You couldn't make money off it. I took the position of *Well, I'm going to run this like a business anyhow.*

To do that, I needed to go back to the white board with the arbitrage team. I spent a lot of time—including nights and weekends—getting our arbitrage models right. I worked with Ed Cotler and John Davi from research, making sure we understood what was going into our prices and our markets. *I'm going to be a market maker,* I said to myself. *I'm going to stand on both sides, I'm going to be a buyer and a seller. I won't make much money initially, but I'll start to build volume so that as the number of trades goes up, I'll see more information, I'll be in the mix. I'll get educated as we go, and that's how I'll build the business.*

That approach later helped me as an entrepreneur: you don't spend years planning to build a business. You do it. You just go in and get wet. As you splash around, you learn where the deeper spots are, the shallower spots, the eddies that you want to avoid. You figure out your edge and find out where you'll make money.

For my arb operation, I had a direct line to a floor trader on the Chicago Mercantile Exchange (CME), Danny Riley. Danny was my guy in Chicago—an outside broker, which was unusual, but I needed a different way of doing things. I wanted to use instant messaging, I wanted to use the phone, and I wanted to be able to switch back and forth. The Merrill guys in the CME pits didn't like that. They wouldn't have given me the level of service I wanted. It took me a couple of months to figure out that I had to go outside the firm and do it on my own. Looking back, that was rare, and my boss, Jarrod, must have gone to bat for me. Also, the Merrill floor trader clearly must not have thought the flow would be significant from my book—oops. That turned out to be their mistake.

On a typical day, I was getting ready for the opening by

preparing my positions. By the time the bell rang, I had my first set of moves scripted, like the opening drive in a football game. I worked on new models and new research as the day went along. I adjusted models. I researched, researched, researched, and researched. I mapped events, looking for catalysts like takeovers or major shifts in regulation that caused prices to change. I would try to find a compelling catalyst and structure a trade to capture those dislocations that may only last for seconds. To Jenn and many of my friends, this sounds incredibly stressful and high stakes, but I was wired to think this way from an early age. We each have our own gifts. Running my trading book was a lifelong dream come true.

Many market events happen every year like clockwork. Traders think ahead for those: *I've got three weeks until* x, *I can arbitrage that event; I need to get my trades ready because I don't want to be in a rush.* Then there are things that just pop up, like the catalyst we found around a change in Microsoft's dividend payout. You see something like that and say to yourself, *I know that in the past special dividends from Microsoft have caused confusion. Let's see if this one does the same.*

That year the Street was unsure how to treat the Microsoft dividend announcement from the perspective of the index. Eddie Cotler, John Davi, and I ran some numbers and realized that the Street's position was wrong. Then we did the usual ton of due diligence. We analyzed the data to understand what the pricing movement was going to be, then we back-tested it. Next, we researched what was going to happen if we got it wrong, what we could lose. I always needed to know how much of a loss I could weather. We could lose, but if we lost a tolerable amount knowing we had the opportunity of a large upside, we still were making a good trade. We figured out the likelihood of being wrong with a calculation of upside versus downside. If the upside was better than 4:1, or whatever ratio the head of the desk was comfortable with, you put the trade on.

After doing our homework for about a week, we were confident that we were right. We lobbied management to take a big position on this index arbitrage trade—to put a substantial amount of money into the trade. We saw that the price of the future was wrong because everyone thought the dividend was going to be treated one way. We knew it was going to be treated exactly the opposite way. That was our edge: we wanted to sell the futures contract (an obligation to sell the NASDAQ 100 at a certain price in three months), and buy (go long) the one hundred stocks in the NASDAQ 100 index. The futures contract was mispriced too high. Of course, we wanted to take a bigger position because we were absolutely convinced that we knew what was going to happen. We grabbed Jarrod Yuster and said, "Look, here's the trade, here's what we want to do. Our risk limit is x, we want to do $4x$ or $5x$." We knew what the potential losses and gains were, so this was limited risk.

I said, "Whatever the market will take, I want to sell. I want the position. I want it in our book." Eddie and I made the case, with John backing us up. Management allowed us to double our position. It was the first time we had asked. We had always played within the risk cap; we had never really taken a swing before. I was disappointed that we didn't get to do it bigger, but it was a matter of timing: this was just before a new manager joined us, and we started to transition into taking bigger positions with more risk.

Two days later, NASDAQ made the announcement, and the NASDAQ future dropped like a stone relative to the stocks in the index. We made $300,000 with no market risk. We were 94 percent of the trade, meaning that we held 94 percent of the short positions open in the NASDAQ futures, which is not a heavily traded contract. It wasn't a huge win financially, but when you're at 94 percent of the volume of a trade on a high-profile stock like Microsoft that everybody's watching, and the information is supposed to be perfect, it's a good thing. We were the only ones on the Street that got it right. Goldman got it wrong, Barclays got it wrong, Bank of America got it wrong . . . all the big arbitrage players got it wrong. These are guys that we traded with every day. Nailing it perfectly brought us credibility.

As we dove into index arbitrage, we learned quickly. At one point, our book was valued at $6 billion. By my fourth year running the index arbitrage book, we were second or third on the Street in index arbitrage, volume-wise, and on my biggest day we were responsible for 9 percent of the total volume of S&P 500 stocks traded that day. That was a good day.

Those days, I found it a minor annoyance to attend to the body's requirements. A lot of people look forward to lunch, but for a trader it's a necessary distraction. It was rarely more than a quick bite. Later in my career, I would go out to lunch occasionally to meet with a broker or to celebrate something. I would start the lunch with "Oh, so this is what people do at twelve o'clock." Like most traders, lunch for me went this way: "Will you watch the screens for me, I'm going to hit the head and grab lunch." I would come back in five minutes with sushi or a sandwich. That's just the way it was.

Typically at about two o'clock I started to get ready for the Close. The Market on Close, or MOC, is the opposite of the MOO and much more important. It's the most critical price of the day— the one that traders want to make sure gets done properly. The MOC is an auction that starts at 3:20 p.m., with indications at 3:20, 3:40, and 3:50.

The indications tell you how many buyers and sellers there are for individual stocks. If there is an imbalance, prices are going to move (remember, nothing more here than the law of supply and demand). In that case the trader might want to provide some liquidity, especially if you've wanted to exit a large position for a while.

A lot of times the computer did that for you, but sometimes you adjusted manually, especially when you saw a big imbalance. You'd say, *Okay, I'm going to step into that liquidity*, or *I'm going to pull right back here because I'm going to move the price on this one and I don't want to do that*. If there are a lot of buyers and you have a lot to sell, you can come in and get rid of that stock quickly and easily, satisfying your sellers without moving the market. Remember that your job as a trader is to sneak in and sneak out and try to move the market as little as possible. If you're impacting the market, you're not doing your job very well.

Every quarter there's what's called quadruple witching, the best time to move a lot of volume quietly. It's a funny name that sounds spooky, and it can be—you can make a mint, or you can lose your shirt. Quadruple witching takes place when four things expire: single stock options and futures, and index options and futures. The index rebalances occur then too, so if stocks are going into the S&P 500, they go in at the closing price on that witching day. Everything expires at the price on the Close.

Because trading volume is at a peak during quadruple witching, there is tremendous liquidity. As an investor, you're saying to yourself, *Okay, if I have a lot of stock to sell, I'm going to sell it on that day because I will have less impact*. Those are busy days. You prepare for them for weeks. The huge volume and movement in price presents opportunities to make money as well as for dislocation— for mistakes to be made. You must identify where those mistakes are, capitalize on them, and make money for your customers and the firm. Quadruple witching provides cover to move larger and more volatile trades.

After the Close, it's all about clearing the stocks, clearing trades, and making sure that they all hit the tape. You need to make sure that customers get their orders quickly, that all the accounts are balanced properly, and that the profit and loss for the day are calculated. By 4:30 or 4:40 p.m. each day, you know how much money you made. All the product side trades are calculated, the salespeople's commissions are calculated, it all gets molded into one big P&L spreadsheet and goes up to senior management. By about six o'clock, you're typically done with your research. Then you go to a bar or out to dinner with a client or with a broker or your colleagues.

By the time I had been trading for a couple of years, I had my computer set up at home with Bloomberg so that after I got home I could make trades in Asian, European, or even African markets—I only made trades in African markets a couple of times, though.

I frequently got phone calls at two in the morning from a broker saying, for example, "Hey Rich, it moved a percent, what do you want me to do—sell it, leave it, buy more?" Money got made at all hours. At that point I was thirty-one and I needed, what, four hours' sleep to get going. I still wasn't drinking coffee, so I wasn't caffeinated; I was working out every morning; I was a machine. Perhaps you can relate to that sense of being at the peak of your powers in your youth and wanting it to last forever. Like an athlete having a career year, I hoped I could stay in the zone as long as possible. The stamina and appetite for risk required as a trader would later prove valuable to me as an entrepreneur creating the global market of disability.

CHAPTER SIXTEEN
THE PHYSICS OF MARKETS

W hen I joined Merrill, the traditional trading desk was dying. The portfolio trading team was tasked with building the automated system that would represent a new era in stock trading. The idea is simple. If a house can understand the risks of a portfolio of stocks as opposed to the individual stocks, it can consolidate the number of traders required and be able to give customers better prices and execution, not to mention making more money for shareholders. Every house on the street was racing to improve automation, and Merrill was starting in last place.

Until the early 2000s, successful traders had to have an intimate knowledge of each stock. They had a book of stocks, perhaps twelve of them. If a trade came onto the desk to sell IBM, say a million shares, it would get routed to the trader who traded IBM. The trader was the house expert. She either decided to keep that in her book or sell it to the market. That trader was uniquely qualified to make that call because she knew what IBM was up to, she understood what was coming down the pipe, she understood the earnings, she understood the fundamentals of the stock. So if one trader can trade twelve stocks and Merrill needed to cover two thousand stocks around the world, that's a lot of people. Now think how all those stocks behave differently—or not. The reality is you've got positions in two thousand stocks that move in similar and different ways to create an entire portfolio for a trading position in Merrill's book.

Trading on a stock-by-stock basis across fifty or a hundred traders is just not an efficient way of doing business. To understand how automation fixes that, you must understand how trading works. At its most basic level, trading is buying or selling stock. A trader's job is not to hold stock but to exit a position, with zero position being normal. What determines how a trader exits is what the transaction to exit will cost. Most people don't understand this. They think traders are just buying, selling, taking a profit. That's called market making, but we were doing more than just that.

On most occasions, we bought risk from clients—meaning clients paid Merrill a certain amount to take stock off their hands. Let's say a pension plan fund manager calls up and says, "I have a position of one million shares of McDonald's that I want you to buy." The fund manager is calling all his contacts on Wall Street. He's calling Goldman, he's calling Merrill, he's calling J.P. Morgan. He's shopping the McDonald's shares to see which bank will give him the best price. If Goldman says that they will charge seven cents a share worth ten dollars to take that onto their book, J.P. Morgan says they will do it for six cents and Merrill says it will cost twelve cents, J.P. Morgan wins the trade. J.P. Morgan has now assumed a risk priced at six cents per share for a million shares of McDonald's stock at ten dollars, meaning J.P. Morgan will have to sell their position at a cost of less than six cents per share to make a profit. That's how trading works, and it was being done on a stock-by-stock basis everywhere in the world. The inefficiency wasn't purposeful; the technology to consolidate everything simply didn't exist at the time. Computers and data modeling changed all that. Trading houses now can consolidate all the risk under a team of a few traders who understand portfolio risk and execution.

With the McDonald's example, the only thing that has changed under automation is that instead of two people on the phone, now it's machine to machine. Each house builds risk limits into its trading system, and the trade goes to whoever is willing to take the most risk. The algorithm centralizes a risk formula for each bank, which takes the human factor largely out of the equation. For example, rather than having a trader calling up the Exchange and saying, "I need to sell twenty million shares of stock x slowly," the trader asks the software to split it up based on an algorithm that analyzes how much stock x typically trades in volume and pattern throughout the day and how much it will impact the market.

Merrill had hired Mike Stewart to start building the automated trading system for the bank. That was a big jump for Mother Merrill, and even more so for Mike and the team that came over with him. They came from a smaller investment house, tasked with reinventing equity trading at Merrill.

Mike wanted to lead the world. He was ready to turn Merrill's tiny portfolio trading desk into the number one portfolio trading desk on the Street. Automation had changed financial trading floors across the world. Banks reduced their trading desks from eighty traders to three. They could manage a book better and more efficiently with three risk traders, robust data, and computer-based algorithms. System engineers baked a deep understanding of risk and historical data into the system that was going to be more efficient than hoping that individual traders collectively understood their smaller, often correlated books. Trading is about understanding what risk you want to keep, what you want to exit, and how much you're willing to pay to do both.

To increase our level of automation, we had to build from the ground up. That took technologists, teammates who understood risk, and people who understood our customers. It was a unique crew of people. It included three or four young guys like me, fresh out of school, hungry to make an impact. We could not have done the job without Rick Jesse, a technologist who understood coding and what it took to build systems that would handle massive amounts of data. We had a database of every trade, bid, and ask for the last twenty years. That's the very definition of big data. It's called a tick database, and it was all new to me at the time. I didn't know anything about market microstructure. I had studied derivatives, I knew risk, but I had no idea about technology.

Mike and Jarrod set me to work. Because I was working so closely with the data, I was learning how to view risk through a market microstructure lens—an entirely unique way of looking at the market. It was like learning about physics for the first time.

Stocks tend to trade in patterns over the course of the six-and-a-half-hour trading day. If you break that day into increments of seconds, half seconds, and milliseconds, those patterns tend to persist. When you are watching TV and you see a sell price go by, there can be as many as one hundred thousand data points behind it. Literally. Most people, I think 99.99 percent of people, don't understand that. Many traders don't understand that. If somebody changes their bid/ask, it creates a data point. If a trade goes through, it creates a data point—an uptick, a downtick, or a zero tick. Every tick affects the market in some way. Ticks are to markets what atomic structure is to matter. There's a pattern, there's a structure, there's a way that ticks in a trade make up the body of a given stock on any given day. Patterns change second by second, depending on what's going on with the stock. You can structure a trade using those patterns to make them efficient for the customer. Before I learned about market microstructure, I only saw the Open and the Close, not the billions of tick points in between.

Jarrod taught me how all this worked. By dealing with this reality of billions and billions and billions of ticks, I was learning what made the market tick, pun intended. For me, the complexity was mind-blowing. I had never seen this before. The six-and-a-half-hour trading day became a thousand trading days. I could now look at the trading day in five-minute, two-minute, one-hour increments. I could look at it in one-second increments, I could look at it in one-millisecond increments. I could tell you about patterns that stay relatively stable in any of those increments. You know the expression "don't miss the forest for the trees"? This is kind of like looking at the cellular level of a tree.

During my first six months at Merrill, I was mostly data testing, which may sound like a menial task, but it was the best way to learn. I had never coded before, but soon I was coding in R, a language for manipulating big data. I was testing for bugs in the code and making sure that the data we were producing matched risk profiles.

While we were doing this, we had to manage the day-to-day work of producing daily trades and risk profiles and research for clients. Not that we were doing much volume. The little that we were doing was manual and very work-intensive. We had to build both the portfolio trading data and the system from scratch: there was nothing there. At the time, nobody was looking at market microstructure except some quants, whom traders dismissed as eggheads. Then the eggheads took over. The timing was perfect from my perspective. Now financial markets are analyzed primarily based on their microstructure, particularly the equity and debt markets. Trades are based on statistical patterns discovered and managed by computers. Traders don't manually try to unwind their big block trades anymore—they walk in silently and use market microstructure to layer in liquidity.

The systems parsed hundreds of billions of data points and spotted trends in a few milliseconds. The three other guys on the team were all computer and mathematics whiz kids from MIT: Ed Cotler, Mark Rosen, and Ira Gerhardt, one of the few holdovers from the old desk. Automated trading was beginning to revolutionize the financial sector, and it was the clients who were going to benefit. They just wanted to get their trades done quickly and efficiently. The cost of trading a stock went from five cents a share to less than a penny. Looking back now, it is painfully obvious that before automation, we had been dividing risk up in a highly inefficient way. We had positions—based on risk profiles—that may at times have been identical across different desks. Managing them on a desk-by-desk basis was highly inefficient.

Consolidating that risk, that flow, was critical to making more money for the bank and more money for Merrill shareholders. With risk consolidated to one channel, you had a global perspective. You could see that cash had a position in IBM, derivatives had a position in IBM, and Portfolio Trading had a position in IBM. That would allow you to decide the best moves from a bank perspective rather than a desk perspective. Before automation, if the cash desk was buying IBM and the derivatives desk was shorting IBM, the bank had canceled out having a position in IBM, but it was very difficult to know that from a macro perspective.

The ultimate result: lower cost of trading and better execution for the investor. Some might wonder why banks would act to shrink their own revenue base by cutting spreads and commission. The competitive forces drove technology to eliminate costs and increase the fight for market share. What banks lost in margin, they made up in volume and lower headcount.

About this time, Phil Lonergan came from London to take over the portfolio trading desk from Jarrod. Under Jarrod we had reached our technology goal. We were ready to expand trading, so Phil's focus was on building our ability to take more and better risks. Jarrod maintained his focus on automated execution, splitting our team off to focus on risk trading. Phil built his career at Deutsche Bank, a bank that had more of a risk culture, so he knew what it would take to turn us into a well-oiled machine in terms of technology and a culture of taking appropriate risk. He was also an exceptional manager—the best boss I ever had, bar none.

Now, I know what this talk about ramping up risk sounds like in a historical context. You're thinking, *Oh, Merrill was ramping up risk right before the Street blew up.* But the two have nothing to do with one another. What caused the issues at Merrill, along with Lehman, in 2008 was the credit derivatives book, not the equity book. This new model—that of taking on additional risk to make money for our shareholders—primarily came from the observed success of Goldman Sachs. The Goldman model worked. It was successful and still is. Unfortunately, Merrill's fixed-income managers didn't understand the risk involved in the positions they had—and it sank the company. They had positions in the credit derivatives book that were . . . I think the technical risk-management term would be "stupid." At the end of the day, traders and those with oversight of those traders—including regulators—did not understand what risks were in their books. It is not illegal—or immoral—to be stupid. Make no mistake, the market failure of 2008 was not caused by greed or widespread fraud—it was caused by a colossal failure of risk management.

Phil spearheaded our new proprietary trading team that traded to protect and enhance Merrill's capital. His job was dismantling the barriers to risk-taking and ensuring that we took smart risks. Eddie went to Columbia to get his MBA, and at that point Phil and I moved up to a new trading area on the ninth floor that was physically separated from the customer side, with fifty other team members. We had no visibility into customer books or trades, and we didn't interact with any Merrill Lynch analysts at all. The Street serviced us as a hedge fund. We had Goldman, J.P. Morgan, Bear Stearns, Lehman Brothers, and others come in to cover us as a fund.

Until then, our trading had always been more about client flow—doing what was right for the client, no matter what. Now that Merrill shareholders were the client, we followed our own best judgment. Phil and I got into some interesting culture clashes. We went from a culture that was not focused on profit to one where every dollar mattered. That meant dismantling fiefdoms where people made a living by protecting their turf. I remember one day we found $10 million of our profit sitting in somebody else's book, seventeen floors up. We had to fight to take it away from this group. Merrill had never had that rigor before. It went from a culture of "ah, don't worry about it" to "every dollar counts."

Phil and I spent a lot of time after hours hanging out together. Phil liked a bar called Eight Mile Creek. It was an Aussie bar and Phil was an Aussie, so I guess it felt like home. Phil had spent some time as a professional rugby player in Australia—and the picture in your mind is pretty close to reality—but dressed for a different kind of battle. One day after the Close, I was heading there to meet up with Phil and Eddie. It was a beautiful day, and I was driving my scooter through Soho. I was stopped at a light at the corner of Spring and Mott when I heard giggling behind me. I turned to see this group of women looking at me.

One of them comes up and, in a British accent, goes, "We love your wheels, can we go for a ride?" There were six of them. I'm thinking, *Sure, what the hell,* so I strike up a conversation with them, and they obviously had had a few too many cocktails, and it turns out they're part of the flight crew of a Virgin Atlantic 747.

I'm dressed in my uniform—slacks and a button-down shirt—and I look pretty good, if I do say so myself. I say, "All right, all six of you, jump on the scooter."

I had one woman in the basket, one in my lap, one on each armrest, and two on the back. At that very moment a fire truck pulls up, and the firefighters are wearing these expressions like *Who's this guy in the scooter with six gorgeous women draped all over him—what is going on?* The siren wails, one of them snaps a picture, the girls are enjoying themselves, and I'm thinking, *Oh no, I need to bring these guys to the bar. I've got to have proof that this really happened.* The bar is about three blocks north. Here I am doing all I can to get these six women to come with me to the bar. I'm chatting them up, speeding along—but about a block and a half away from the bar, they get bored and take off.

By this time, I'm about twenty minutes late. I'm never late, right? So I get to the bar and Phil immediately goes, "What happened to you?"

"Do I have a story for you," I tell him. "The problem is, I can't prove it happened."

I told the story, and they died laughing, of course. Eddie said, "Rich, that's awesome! Too bad you have no proof." It still bothers me that somewhere out there there's an FDNY fireman who I can't find with a picture on his phone of me and half of a 747 flight crew rolling up Mott Street.

CHAPTER SEVENTEEN
REBRANDING DISABILITY

When you join a firm from a university, you typically join the recruiting team for your school. You don't have to do it; you choose to because you love the school, you love the firm, you're a climber, and you want to boost your career. I got involved because I thought the system was brilliant. And as you can tell, I have a lot of time for Columbia.

Every year, I was going back to Columbia to find the best of the best for Merrill. Of course, we had all played the recruiting game ourselves, very recently, so we knew exactly how this worked. It wasn't like we had to be trained to do this. The only difference was that instead of selling yourself, you're selling the company. When you know all the students a year behind you, you generally have an idea of who you want to go after.

We started recruiting in early September, sometimes late August. The quicker we could get to campus, the better. We had to find the best in the class and convince them to come to Merrill rather than Goldman, J.P. Morgan, or anywhere else. Merrill had separate recruiting teams for Columbia, Harvard, Wharton, University of Chicago, NYU—all the top schools.

Recruiting followed the cycle I experienced at Columbia, starting with large events including every business and then sequencing into smaller settings as each department zeroed in on its top recruits over the course of the fall. After two or three events, Merrill ended up with sixty to a hundred people for all four businesses. From Columbia we expected to hire at least five or six graduates a year to join the sales and trading department. It would probably be the same number from Wharton, from Harvard, and so on.

By about year four at Merrill, I was comfortable enough with my success as a trader and had seen enough of the recruiting process at Columbia that I started asking myself, *Why the hell aren't we doing this for disability?* I *knew* there were people out there like me. They came to me quietly at these events, saying, "You did this with a disability; don't tell anybody, but I have a disability too. Can you give me some advice on how to handle it?" Sometimes they would name it: a learning disability, dyslexia, ADD, dysgraphia, depression, bipolar. And it's funny: I never cared what the condition was. All that mattered was that it was a disability that the individual identified with.

This was happening to me quite a bit—in fact, more than once per event. Merrill's diversity recruiting team came along with us when we went to campus. They would ask us to identify high-performing women and high-performing people of different races. That was the focus at the time. It dawned on me that I needed to get people with disabilities into the recruiting conversation. I stuck up my hand and said, "Hey, guys, we are missing an opportunity here with people with disabilities. Is there something we can do as a firm to focus on closing the gap?"

There was an effort afoot at Merrill to include parents of kids with disabilities in an employee resource group, or ERG. I had a good relationship with the man leading the charge— Charlie Hammerman, director of equity capital markets—and he was pushing me to get more involved. Charlie had been part of the effort to recruit me to Merrill. I was quickly recruited into that effort as one of the few people with a disability in a high-performing business position. I never quite understood those efforts. They seemed to me to be, at best, a parallel track to Merrill's business interests. More of a human-interest story than anything else. While that was not the intent, it was the result. These ERG efforts were still in the realm of doing good, of charity, even though there was just a hint of business value. I saw that they were not fully recognizing the potential of the disability market. What they were doing with disability was not in the same league as what they were doing with women and with race. And then there was the problem of, well, how do you get a company that doesn't understand disability to do this right?

Around that time, I started working with a woman named Susan Lang. She represented a group out of Tampa called Enable America and was interested in the idea of disability recruiting. Susan and I hit it off immediately. She asked me to come in and speak to the team about this recruiting concept over a period of three or four months.

I flew to Tampa to meet with them a few times and eventually brought my dad down. The group wanted to figure out what they wanted to be when they grew up, and Dad is an expert in strategic planning. We went to a hotel in Tampa for the weekend with their senior management team and we took them through a strategic planning process. The output of that session later became Lime Connect in 2006—but Enable America as an organization decided they would not join the direction discussed at the meetings. Susan and I decided to start our own organization outside of the traditional charity advocacy model. I was looking for something real, something concrete, something based on merit. I didn't want to do the Beltway two-step—I was looking for a business-driven philosophy. Apolitical. Enable America wasn't interested, but the experience got me thinking more and more about how to do disability right from a business context.

While all of this was going on, I had been getting calls at work from this disability group and that disability group and any number of charities and political groups based largely in Washington, DC, wanting to draft me onto their boards. Getting these calls was torture. You already knew what they wanted. I was a successful guy, well spoken, making money, ideal for a directorship at one of these charity groups. I was kind of a unique commodity, I guess you could say. If their board of directors was already flushed out, they wanted money. "Oh, you're a disabled trader," they would hint. Translation: "I want some money, I want a $10,000 check."

As I met with these people and started to understand how these charities work, I saw they didn't want to change. Their horizon is three months' survival. That's the sad part. These charities don't have the capacity to change things. They're trying to survive; they're looking for the next donor. I understand that. It makes total sense to me. But it's not what people think it is. These are not vehicles for change. They want to fund a model that enables them to sustain operations.

As a society we celebrate speeches, but change doesn't happen at the podium. You can't give a speech and call it change. Speeches can help inspire change, but real change is what people, institutions, companies, and governments do on the ground every day. That's what causes change, and it's what's missing in those charities. They're all fluff. If you examine their mandates, they're not really interested in changing a damn thing. The phone calls I was receiving reinforced that, but I have seen this stasis from inside as well. I accepted a few of these offers, both to see if I could have an impact and to learn from the inside what was really going on. It is still a tactic I use today—if I want to understand a process, I join the process. I had a fiduciary duty as a member of several charity boards to try and change these organizations. And I failed. I failed to instigate the change required to materially improve the lives of PWD. These organizations are doing almost the same things that they were doing in the 1960s. No change. No difference made. They dial for dollars to keep the lights on and to maintain their status quo. The change that they advocate for requires a radically different approach that they are unable to even articulate, much less act to create.

I don't know about you, but if I had an employee that had a job for thirty years and they hadn't made any progress, I'd fire the employee. *I* should be fired for waiting thirty years to fire *him*. And yet, despite an almost complete lack of progress, these organizations still get funded. This is amazing to me. For decades we have had the same organizations and processes in place that produce little in the way of measurable results, funded to the tune of $300 billion a year in the U.S., and the debate isn't about whether to change them. The debate is whether to increase funding. What? Are you guys silly? No wonder nobody wants to touch this space. People take one look and go, "Why the hell would I want to spend the next ten years unraveling this quagmire?"

I want to see these groups change dramatically. I think they have a role to play; I think they could be producing a lot more benefit than they are currently. The problem is, it takes a radical change for any of these organizations to get out of their own way. What is more likely to happen is guys like me coming out of universities and a career in business, having a disability and starting their own new groups. Which I did. But for that to happen at the kind of scale needed to matter, people must be convinced that there's a possibility for success.

If you're a smart woman coming out of Stanford or another place that smart people come out of, you're going to take one look at disability and say, *Hmmmm. Technology start-up versus a disability start-up . . . oh my God, no way. I'll take the technology start-up any day. Why would I want to deal with this when I can go over there?*

So, I was having these conversations with Susan at Enable America, thinking maybe I would take a step forward and do something real. Then I had a beer with some Columbia friends, Danny Mayer and Dustin Longstreth and some other people. We were at a bar and the conversation came around to disability somehow. I remember saying, "Yeah, you know, guys, I'm getting all these requests and calls from disability groups, and I did the math and this market looks big. Nobody's really looking at it."

I asked Dustin to share his thoughts on what happened next. His recollection:

> The story that always comes to mind when I think of my early days with Rich is this particular conversation we had at the Old Town Tavern on East Eighteenth Street. We had graduated from business school and were now back out working in the real world. I was starting a new career as a brand strategist (and learning what that even was). Rich was making boatloads of money on Wall Street as a trader—just as he had always planned.
>
> While Rich is an unapologetic capitalist, he is also a bit of an outspoken rebel (with a cause). It was clear that financial success alone would not be enough. There was an itch that he still needed to scratch.
>
> After a few drinks I asked him, "Rich, as a successful young man who happens to have a disability, what type of leader do you want to be? What kind of dent do you want to make in this world?"

He leaned forward, took a long sip of his vodka tonic from a straw (Rich's preferred method of cocktail consumption), looked at me, and said, "I want to rebrand disability."

How's that for ambition?

The brand of disability that the general population had come to know was firmly rooted in shame, pity, charity, or at best the dramatization of heroic efforts to simply function and be "normal." That wasn't Rich's experience at all. He saw something bigger—something that everyone, disability or not, could value and even be amazed by. But in order to get others to see his vision, he needed to get them to think in a radically different way about the brand of disability.

He's been on that journey ever since.

This moment is when the light went on for me. That was the inflection point. It was an epiphany, pure and simple. That was the first time I remember thinking, *Game on. Let's go have some fun.* I didn't know what that looked like, I had no idea we would end up where we are, but I was ready to get in the game. Shortly after that, either Susan said to me or I said to Susan, "To get this done, we need to start an organization from scratch." There was just too much muscle memory in existing organizations. They would be impossible to change. I said, "Look, I can't pay you, but let's give it a shot." Susan left her job and we started Lime Connect.

Susan has a background in not-for-profit marketing and a strong grasp of market forces and is always customer-focused, which is why we became fast colleagues. She has the ability to cut through rhetoric, and there is always an abundance of rhetoric in disability. Susan's biggest strength is that she gets things done. In a space where there are many "talkers," Susan is a "doer."

To her credit, Susan joined, despite our lack of funding. This was near the end of 2005. We decided that we were going to create an organization that runs recruiting events with large corporations on campuses, as was being done for women, except that we would focus on disability. This organization we were going to build would enable companies to simply show up and pick candidates. All the work would be done for them. It's minimal risk, it's easy to understand, it's value-added. You show up, you see great people, you make the hire . . . everybody's happy. That was the concept that became Lime.

I started the process of selling the idea to Merrill. They loved it. Merrill was the first one in the pool, with $125,000 year one to get it started. But we couldn't do it with just Merrill. I didn't need a salary, I had an excellent job, but Susan needed to make a living. We needed money to travel, to build a brand, and to sell the concept. We had to find other partners.

By this time, I had built a good relationship with PepsiCo. That had started a couple of years earlier, when I was sitting at the desk one day on the fifth floor and I got a phone call from Stan O'Neal's office, the CEO of Merrill Lynch. "Look, Rich," he said, "I need you to do me a favor. We want to do more business with PepsiCo on their pension side and then their banking side. Their CEO called me the other day asking what we are doing that's so great in disability. I'm told you're pretty good at speaking on this topic. Would you mind going up to Purchase and talking to them about what we do at Merrill, how it works, what we're planning for the future, and how we're going to tackle it."

Stan O'Neal's office knew about me because a couple of months earlier I had testified in Washington in front of the Equal Employment Opportunity Commission, or the EEOC, on what working for Merrill Lynch with a disability was like and how I had become successful there. I had never seen that Washington world before. I was picked up by limousine, shown around the city, taken to a government office to testify, and whisked away back to the airport. It was a very positive experience.

I went up to Purchase, New York, to speak on behalf of Merrill Lynch. I was thirty years old at this point. It was the kickoff of PepsiCo's Disability Employee Resource Group. They had about thirty people in the room trying to figure it out. I talked about some of the things that we knew, some of the things that worked for Merrill, some of the things that didn't work very well—kind of a confidence-building eye-opener.

That was 2005. It was the start of a long journey with PepsiCo. When we were starting Lime Connect (I will explain how we came up with the name shortly), PepsiCo was a natural second call. We explained that our product was based on what every major company in America does in their campus recruiting. It was the same product with a disability twist. If you walked into one of our recruiting events at the University of Texas, at Columbia, at the University of Toronto, you would know that everybody in the room had a disability. You didn't have to ask. You just knew it. So that was obviously very attractive to Pepsi. They wanted to get into this area that was underserved. Pepsi became our second founding partner after Merrill, at $125,000 per year.

Susan was running the day-to-day operations; I supported her with sales and strategic help. We eventually landed Goldman Sachs, and we landed Google. Pepsi took us four months to land; Google took us two weeks. No surprise there: we were talking the same language of innovation. Google calls themselves a technology company, but really they're not. They are an innovation company. If it's a new thing and a big market, they will go there. As an aside, a lot of the innovation that Google undertakes serves disability. Google Glass, the Google self-driving car—the majority of the Google X projects fit right in with disability.

We wanted Lime to create actions that moved numbers a lot— to inject talented people into great companies. The rest is up to the companies. By changing their behavior, they turn the new talent they hire into lifelong assets. The key to success for Lime: this wasn't about support. We wanted to be as far away from support as we could possibly get. We wanted to focus on career success. We didn't choose this direction because we had crunched the numbers or tested it on focus groups; we did it initially because it worked for me as a person with a disability, and I was hearing the same from others I had met at Merrill recruiting events. I assumed that there were millions of people with similar experiences out there. I had no statistical basis for it; I was going on gut feel—to start. That's how most first steps are taken—an educated gut feeling.

About six months after we started Lime Connect and started having campus recruiting events, we did some customer research. We started talking to the students on campus to find out why they were so attracted to what we were doing. Because it was a hit. The messaging we used was "success first, disability second." It resonated. The students loved it. They were flocking to events. We literally had to close the doors. In one case, so many people wanted to come into the room that we were creating a fire hazard. These students had never been asked to join these firms within the context of disability.

We went to all the campuses where our corporate partners recruited. Merrill, Goldman, Google, and Pepsi picked all the top schools: Chicago, Columbia, Harvard, Georgetown, University of Texas, Stanford, Berkeley . . . all the schools where they typically recruited, there we were.

I asked Danny Mayer and Dustin Longstreth to join the board of Lime Connect, and they quickly proved amazing leaders. Dustin got us to this brand name. He understands how to build and maintain a popular brand. At that point he was working with some of the best brands in the world. We were all four years out of university and had a footing in our own world. His world was branding. So he took us through a process of understanding what our customers wanted, the customers being any student on campus who happened to have an identity as a person with a disability. We already knew what the corporations wanted—great people.

The students wanted to focus on their careers. They were already successful people—they had gotten into the best schools in the world—and they wanted to extrapolate that success into the business world, whether it be banking, technology, or consumer packaged-goods companies like PepsiCo. The feedback we were getting seems obvious now, but it was diametrically opposed to where disability groups were at that point. They were reveling in disability. And in doing that, they were turning off the best talent. Because the best talent wanted to be known for what they were good at, not for their disability.

People with disabilities don't come home and watch *Disability Tonight*. They watch *Entertainment Tonight*. But if you put a bit of a twist on *Entertainment Tonight* and you include Marlee Matlin, Aimee Mullins, or some other star with a disability, they will pay closer attention. And they will get excited by it. That philosophy applies to almost every other non-traditional market. You take what people want and you put a twist on it. Amp up the connection with disability by making subtle hints and sometimes not-so-subtle hints. But don't dive deep. That's not how most people live their lives.

When I am walking down the street, I don't see myself as a disabled guy. I see myself as a father who has unfortunately fallen in love with the Toronto Maple Leafs and happens to have a disability. It's a subtle distinction. But the way that the public views me is very different—it's disability first. But that's not the way that a person with a disability handles identity.

I didn't come up with the identity piece myself—I had never thought it through. Dustin helped me think it through. He understands how consumer identity works because he studied it. Identity applies as well to a person with a disability as to any homogenous group with similar traits and life experiences. That has never actually been thought about in disability in a market context. Ever. I think we were the first to really look at that, to really apply market rigor to this vertical.

I'm talking about this now because that was the mantra of Lime: success first, disability second. What we were discovering was essentially buying behavior, but buying into joining brands like Goldman Sachs or Google or Merrill Lynch or PepsiCo rather than buying products. The same triggers apply. It was all about "buying" or connecting with a brand, which is why we called it Lime Connect.

Dustin introduced us to a group called United Design that took us through a naming exercise, directly linked to an encompassing brand identity. My instructions to the team were simple. I said, "I want you to get me as far outside of disability as you can. I don't want people to think of this as being about disability. We're about talent, we're about success, we're about career. That happens to come with disability. Go." And they came back with identities that were unique.

Here's an inside tip: if you ever hire a branding company, the idea they give you last is always the one that they want you to pick. So they gave us five or six names, all with logos and graphics—the tools to create brand identity. On the last page was a bright green circle with the word "Lime" in the middle of it. I looked at it and thought, *What the heck is this?* I didn't say that out loud, but it's what I was thinking. I hated it. They were presenting it to us in a boardroom off the trading floor of the Merrill Lynch offices. After the meeting I went back to my desk on the floor and thought, *What the hell did I just see? That was terrible!* And then I realized that my instructions to these guys had been "Get me as far outside of disability as you can." Which is exactly what they did with Lime. And I instantly fell in love with it. I went from hating it one second to a realization of *No, that's exactly what I want!* After a tricky process of convincing Susan and the board that this name was the best way forward, Lime was born.

CHAPTER EIGHTEEN
NEW HORIZON

T he idea of Return on Disability, or RoD, came into my head in late 2007, almost two years after Lime was born. I was already halfway out the door at Merrill. It was becoming increasingly clear that the market was changing, and that business was not going to be very good for the three years ahead of us. It turned out to be the Great Recession, but you couldn't have known that at the time. I guess I made the right call. I was bearish, and I was one of the few portfolio managers on the team calling for the market to drop. I can remember the head of our desk, Adam Savin, going around the room at one of our morning meetings asking, "Is the S&P going to be up one hundred points or down one hundred points in the next twelve months?" Just to test the sentiment, I said, "Down three hundred."

Everyone booed.

Even I thought I was too bearish, though I was surprised that I was the only one who would express it publicly. I didn't like what I was seeing; the market was not good. A number of us saw the signs that the mortgage market was in free fall. Raul Bhatterjee, the real estate portfolio manager for our team, was seeing outright chaos. I remember him saying that he couldn't put his finger on it, but that something dramatic was changing. I could see some signs even then that the market was going to fall, although I didn't know it would be a full collapse. Things were starting to dislocate, and the market was showing signs of stress. I didn't know how deep we were going to go, but we were going down.

We also didn't know the extent to which Merrill Lynch's positions of collateralized debt obligations (CDOs) would contribute to the collapse and to Merrill's own demise and sale to Bank of America. By the mid-2000s, the big brokerages were competing to build portfolios of credit derivatives linked to the housing boom (a.k.a. policy-incented bubble) in the U.S. The push was part of a shift toward taking more risk that was happening Street-wide. Management at Merrill was no different, correctly diagnosing an opportunity to best serve shareholders by better deploying capital. Their fundamental error was that they did not understand the risks embedded in the portfolio of CDOs, directly linked to failed mortgages.

While I am not writing a book about Merrill's collapse, I think there are key learnings here for non-traditional markets and investors. An investor's job is to manage risk—full stop. The first rule of risk management is to know what risks you are holding. There were portfolios at that time—including Merrill's CDO book—where risk managers either didn't know or ignored the risks that they held. I believe that the same is true for companies and investors that do not understand non-traditional markets—such as women or people with disabilities.

How does that happen? Well, you do it every day. There is a risk that you will get killed in a car accident today. You minimize that risk by wearing a seat belt, not texting while you drive, and taking the car for routine maintenance. Cars are built to protect you from most accidents—but not all. Cars are not designed to drive off cliffs. Due to driver skill and road safety mechanisms, the likelihood of you driving off a cliff is so low that you still drive your car. Risk managers miscalculated the likelihood of CDOs driving off a cliff. The technical word for it is "tail risk," referring to the "tails" or extremes of a normal distribution. Translation— stuff that rarely happens. "Rarely" does not mean "never." Here's a hint: "rarely" happens more often than forecasts predict.

Next time someone tells you that greed caused the Great Recession, feel free to point them to a statistics webinar—and ask them to revisit their political talking points once they understand tail risk. There are valid reasons why the system failed, and the solution lies in better decisions about risk management, rather than goofy former actors and professors grandstanding about greed.

Few were bearish when profits were breaking records between 2006 and 2008—including virtually every analyst on the Street, CNBC, and the entire mainstream financial media. Merrill's issue was not investing aggressively in CDOs per se, but in mistakenly or unknowingly taking on more risk than they could afford to sustain when bad mortgages defaulted. Merrill's managers were hardly alone. A generation of financial experts analyzed data that said mortgages don't default.

As chief investment officer and media personality Barry Ritholtz has written, "Based on a lifetime of observations and a few decades in the markets, I understand that societies, beliefs, and fashions all move in long arcs of time. We call these arcs several things: cycles, periods, eras." Merrill's risk managers failed to anticipate the worst case—tail risk. By the time they understood, their position was so large that they could not cut losses before it was too late. By 2008, the board had fired O'Neal and named John Thain CEO; he negotiated the Bank of America merger, concluding the very same weekend Lehman Brothers collapsed.

While I view the cause of these events as rooted in a colossal failure of market risk management—the ultimate insult for a market professional—some good came out of this dark period. Governance is stronger—boards are asking more and better questions. Regulation is more responsive—although it has become far too onerous. Risk has taken a primary position over revenue in the U.S., catching up to Canada and Europe. All good things for investors.

In retrospect, I look like a genius for leaving Merrill when I did, but the scale of the collapse certainly surprised me. Most traders were thriving on the feverish boom. The one thing about Wall Street and investment, in general, is that there is a natural bias to being bullish. Because when markets go up, almost everybody makes money. Investors are happy. Banks are lending profitably. Investment advisers are earning fees on rising asset levels. Everybody's happy. Remember, during good times on Wall Street, winners make the news—until they don't. You don't read about the guys that lose money unless they do something illegal or colossally stupid. Being a bear is unpopular. It's a sad, sad place to be. It means that people are going to get fired, people are going to lose value in their investments, very few are going to earn economic profit.

When you're losing money and everybody else is losing money too, no big deal. But if you act like it's a bear market and it's not, you're one of the few in the red. If you're losing money and everyone else is making money, that's not fun, right? Bull-versus-bear talk is much more about psychology than economics.

If I hadn't had that big idea in disability, I would still be there. I enjoy trading based on risk, and there were—and still are—roles available to me to continue that passion. But if I was going to take a swing at being an entreprenuer, that was the time to do it. I said to myself, as I'm sure you have at one time or another in your life, *You know what? I'm going to give this my best shot.* The cost of leaving Merrill was at its lowest point.

When I left Merrill in March 2008, Lime was going gang-busters. I was chairman of the board, we were growing through $500,000 on the way to $900,000 in annual revenue, adding new partners, but I knew it was too small for what I wanted to do. One of the things we did to market Lime was to print little factoids on our business cards and marketing collateral. One of them was "Disability is a market the size of China," an insight sparked by research that I had done leveraging U.S. Census data.

That statistic and its implications for the economy and my own future kept me up at night. I also had the understanding—call it ego, call it a nagging sense of responsibility—that I could play a unique role in that marketplace. I can't remember who said it, whether it was my father or whether it was a friend of mine, but somebody asked me, "How many times in life do you get the opportunity to be the leading expert in a market the size of China?" That simple statement was weighing me down like an anchor. I was carrying it with me wherever I went—airports, restaurants, home office. I would see opportunities everywhere to change the world and also to make money . . . I couldn't avoid it.

I asked myself if I wanted to keep working for somebody else. My answer was that if I stayed at Merrill, my earnings would have a ceiling, and so would my impact on the world. In the early days of this financial crisis, my group was being shrunk and collapsed. Merrill had offered me the opportunity to go back to managing the consolidated risk of client-facing activity. Or I could make a clean break. I could start a new business. I had built a brand, developed a model, and saw the market opportunity.

I decided to take my swing. I got a package from Merrill and left the firm.

CHAPTER NINETEEN
CLOSE ENCOUNTERS: FINDING LOVE

W hen I traveled to Tampa in November 2005 to work with Enable America, I ended up hitting it off with one of their employees at the dinner on Saturday night. We closed the bar, and she joined me in my hotel room. I remember thinking, *Oh, okay, so that's how you do that.* That evening solidified for me that I could date and be in the company of a woman.

Just before that weekend, I had picked up a book called *The Game: Penetrating the Secret Society of Pickup Artists.* This little book takes you through the art of attraction as the author picks up dozens of women. It's less than favorable to the female sex because it systematizes the "pickup" and doesn't deal at all with dating or having an actual relationship. I don't agree with or support taking advantage of women in any way, and whatever happens between two people requires mutual consent and a robust mutual enthusiasm about what they do. The sexual harassment revelations in the news in late 2017 made me sick to my stomach. As far as I'm concerned, bosses who take advantage of their authority with female peers and subordinates should be (after due process) immediately fired. Because dating women was new to me and a source of significant anxiety, I needed a process to demystify this formidable mystery. I used the book as a fear remover, nothing more.

That's how I'm wired: I need a process. I had never looked at dating this way before. I had always been wrapped up in a naïve teenage notion that the ideal relationship simply comes into being out of some magical pixie dust. It's the way that a lot of people think about romance, but it ignores some necessary steps that need to happen for a relationship to blossom.

Thanks to *The Game*, I could separate the emotion from the process and realize that dating was merely a numbers game. Most of the book I threw away as junk. I kept one kernel of insight: it's straightforward to meet people if you make a plan to do so. And to find the right person for you, you must meet a whole lot of people. This is especially true for me. The numbers are not in my favor; most people find it remarkably tricky to sort out what disability requires of them—I'm trying to be polite.

I had never dabbled in dating before. It had always seemed too complicated, nerve-wracking, and uncertain, so I had avoided it. I knew that many people with disabilities never go there at all. I wasn't able—in fact, I hadn't even tried—to chunk it out into a process, which is how my brain works. I never leave things to fate. I believe that if you want something, you have to put in the effort and failures to get it. I wanted to have a partner; I hoped to find love. Luckily, at that point in my life, I had built up a good deal of self-confidence. I was a successful trader on Wall Street. I had a bit of a swagger. I knew it was time to get serious about finding a life mate. Once the Tampa romance played itself out, along with the enjoyment and learning that came with it, I committed myself: I was going to meet as many women as I could and find the best partner I could find.

I remember one of my dates, a woman named Kate. She was studying to be a neurosurgeon. We got along well, and we went out three or four times. At the end of the last date, she said, "Look, I like you, but the reality is I don't want to come home and deal with what I deal with at work." That was a fair comment. I didn't particularly like it, but I could understand it. She was a smart, attractive woman who was interesting to me, but she couldn't get past the disability. And that's okay. That's what volume dating is all about. You have to get to a point where it isn't an emotional event; it's just part of the process. In the end, it's a good thing that that happened, because eventually I did find "the one."

To get moving on the dating thing, I joined eHarmony. I was thirty at this point. I was dating to find somebody I enjoyed spending time with, not this elusive, theoretical person that per-haps didn't even exist. I opened myself up, having decided that to do this I had to allow myself to get kicked in the guts repeatedly. I was playing things straight up. No games, just being myself, meeting as many people as I could, and being ready to proceed should things go favorably.

I ended up going out with fifty-four women in fifty-two weeks. You've heard of speed dating? Well, I coined the phrase "volume dating." I had all my first dates in the bar at the Maritime Hotel. It was quiet enough for conversation, easy to get to, upscale, and in a good neighborhood. Usually, that's where it stopped, because there wasn't a fit.

The Maritime was a great venue because I could control the environment and focus on the person sitting across from me. When you have a disability, there are so many moving parts. Plus, you're dealing with affairs of the heart, so there are a lot of other things going on. You want to remove as many variables as you can. Why the hell not, right? You would do that in every other situation.

If the bar went well, I had a go-to restaurant around the corner where we would have dinner. I did that four or five times. I had about a 10 percent success rate advancing to a second date, which was usually dinner or a musical or some event. It could be a gala if she was into that; it could be a museum. It depended on what she wanted to do. Fifty-three potential partners later, I met the right one for me. In November 2006, I met my wife.

Jenn was different from the women I had met to that point. I was very comfortable with her and didn't need to guess what she was thinking. We were having marathon text chats from the get-go. We would instant message from six at night until four in the morning. That was different for me, because I always went to bed at ten—I got up at two in the morning to check Asia, so I tried to get to sleep early. But chatting online was exciting, and my thought was *I'm going to be up soon anyway, so what the hell?* We had a couple of those eight-hour sessions, going back and forth, figuring out what we had in common. We are both market conservatives, so we tend to favor market activity over centralized planning. We are also somewhat liberal in our social views, and our overall values seemed to gel nicely.

When Jenn and I first started IMing, I asked her if she had Googled me. I wanted to let her know that I was a bit different. Thanks to volume dating, I had learned to quickly address disability and "weed out" the ones who could not open their minds. I didn't want to scare her off, but I didn't want to invest a ton of time if the mere thought of a disability was going to end the journey before it started. She wrote "no," and there was a long pause in our chat. Of course, she was typing my name in the search bar.

In my mind's eye, I could see her reading the list of articles that mentioned I happen to have CP. I'll admit, that minute or so seemed longer. Then my smile returned quickly, because she wrote back, "CP—which one is that? Does everything work fine?" I wrote back, "I'm unstoppable," and we kept on chatting. I called her on the second day, after warning her that I had a unique accent, which didn't phase Jenn at all. Things were on track.

I skipped the Maritime Hotel and invited Jenn out to my third-date restaurant in the Village—Freddy's, a family-run place that had great Italian food. It was a little off the beaten path and wasn't an A-list restaurant, but people in the know loved it. I had been going there for probably over a year, both with work people and with dates, so they knew me well. Jenn had never been there, although she went to a bar just around the corner every week with her friends.

The date was November 17, 2006. She met me at my place, and she says that when I opened the apartment door and she saw me standing there, it was like I opened the door to her heart. She says she was acting like a high school girl, giggling uncontrollably. She may be exaggerating a little. When we walked into the restaurant, everyone turned around, of course, because I'm different, so that registered early on for Jenn. And her entrance registered on me.

That was the start of a forty-eight-hour first date. After dinner, Jenn had to go home and take care of her dog, and she asked me to come over. I had been invited to watch a football game at a friend's apartment the next day—Ohio State versus Michigan—so I asked Jenn along. Of course, nobody had met her before. In fact, nobody had met any of my dates before. So here we are, walking into a roomful of my best friends, with me wearing the dress shirt and slacks I had on the day before. Danny Mayer looked me up and down and put two and two together. "Nice shirt, Donovan." Jenn was wearing red, both of us oblivious to what that meant to a crowd of Michigan supporters in the room. Besides Danny and his wife, Tina, Dustin Longstreth was there with his new wife, Kim, and so was Shantha Rau, who would later go on to become the director of disability rights for Human Rights Watch. These are all good friends and at that time were also board members of Lime Connect, which we were just launching. I was into my first three months of running my proprietary trading book at Merrill. It was an intense time.

That first date set the pace. Just a week later, I was over at Jenn's parents' place for Thanksgiving. It was great—nice people—but I was dragging my butt. Getting Lime going, starting this new relationship with Jenn, and running my book all at the same time was taking a toll. Proprietary trading involves taking market risk, unlike the arbitrage book I had been running for four years, where you're taking more discreet kinds of factor risks.

At Christmastime, I brought Jenn up north of Toronto to meet my family. I had flown up to Toronto on business three or four days before the Christmas holidays to assess trading opportunities. I knew Canada better than the Americans that ran large investment pools. I had figured out that I could get trades on up there about two weeks before the Americans knew what was going on. I just let them value the trade for me by getting in ten days before the U.S.-based traders. It is always amazing to me how slowly information flows to U.S. markets from international markets. So much for perfect market theory.

By Christmas Eve I was exhausted. I had been pulling eighteen-hour days for probably three months straight while meeting people and dating. It was intense. We stayed with my family for Christmas Eve, and on Christmas morning we flew back to New York, then drove an hour to get to Jenn's parents' place in time for Christmas dinner. At that point, we had known each other for about six weeks. I had met her parents and her family briefly at Thanksgiving, but I hadn't had a lot of one-on-one time with anyone.

We got to her parents' at about five in the evening, exhausted after traveling the whole day and driving through a snowstorm. When we sat down for dinner, everyone started making a big fuss over the lobster bisque, which is one of Jenn's mom's special holiday dishes. At this point, I'm beyond exhausted. I can barely stand up. So we sit down, Jenn's mom serves the lobster bisque, and I promptly vomit into it. Welcome to the family, eh?

Jenn looked at me in wide-eyed horror and said, "Oh my God . . . are you okay? What the hell just happened?" What happened was my body was rebelling. I just needed to stop. I excused myself and went off to the bathroom, but Jenn's dad didn't skip a beat. He just kept talking—pretended it didn't even happen. He didn't want me to feel bad. But for quite a few years after that, his Christmastime joke never varied: "Hey, Rich, do you want to try the lobster bisque?"

Those first six weeks were quite the introduction. We were in each other's pockets—there were no filters. Jenn and I both just dove into things and never looked back. We also traveled a lot, immediately. We went to Aruba at Valentine's for a couple of days and Northern Ireland in the summer, along with several other quick trips.

Jenn was different than the other women I had dated that year. She had a confidence about her that was tempered by kindness. It was easy to invest time together, and I did not feel the need to edit myself with her. Two weeks into our relationship, she attended a Christmas party at my apartment without knowing more than a handful of people—and charmed everyone. I was hooked.

On June 1, 2007—six months after we met—my lease came up, and we decided to move in together, since Jenn owned her place. This is a common New York City occurrence for young couples with two rents. We ended up staying at the Ritz for about a week because Jenn was having her bathroom renovated. In the end, we had to move my stuff into her place while they were still renovating. I moved from a beautiful, bright space downtown to Jenn's dark little one-bedroom apartment on the Upper West Side. I used to keep my big scooter in the lobby of my apartment building, but there was no room for it at Jenn's. We had to store it at Jenn's parents' place, and I got a crappy little scooter that would fit in the pre-war elevator. But I had this magical woman with me, so that's all that mattered.

Jenn got a quick introduction to my world of disability, and I got a quick introduction to her world of fashion. What she did was fascinating. I loved it because there are a lot of similarities between fashion and the market: trends, what's coming down the pipe, having your finger on the pulse. Like finance, fashion is global. Timing the manufacture, shipping, and sale just right is part art, part science.

Jenn was working at Haskell Jewels, a jewelry manufacturer. She was running product development and merchandising for the launch of Betsey Johnson jewelry, which turned out to be one of the best brands in the business for several years. It was not a perfect fit for her, but she was excited about the opportunity. We both knew that Haskell wasn't a corporate enough environment for her, but Jenn learned a lot there.

One day we were sitting up on Jenn's roof deck with a cocktail, as we sometimes did, and talking about career aspirations. I asked her to write down twenty companies that she admired. "Doesn't matter what industry they're in," I said, "doesn't matter where they're located, just write them down." Jenn had a bachelor of science degree in marketing management from Syracuse University and up until then had spent her career developing jewelry brands in the retail industry. I was trying to get her to think about where she wanted to go next because she was getting tired of fashion. So she wrote them down, and one of the companies at the top of her list was the Food Network. I said, "Why don't you go and apply— they're right downtown." Jenn was not used to stepping out of her comfort zone like this, but she quickly embraced this approach.

Jenn went down to Chelsea, introduced herself to the receptionist at the Food Network, and passed along her résumé. As she was leaving, an executive walked by and engaged her in a quick conversation. This woman took a copy of Jenn's résumé and emailed her later, writing, "I love it that you came down here. I love that you had the guts to do it." Initiative rewarded.

Jenn ended up securing a role managing the jewelry business at Avon Products, one of the companies on her list and a $300 million business. Jenn ran product development, ensuring the right products were chosen and manufactured at the right quality/cost mix. She traveled all over the world. It was perfect.

In fall 2007, Shantha Rau announced that she was getting married to Stefan Barriga, an Austrian who worked for the UN ambassador to Liechtenstein. They were having the wedding in Mysore, India. Shantha is a good friend who was supportive as Lime launched; this was a singular opportunity, so Jenn and I decided to make a two-week trip just before I left Merrill Lynch.

At that point, I had begun thinking about proposing to Jenn, but I wasn't planning on doing it immediately. Then the India trip appeared on the radar, and right away it got me thinking. A first trip to India usually includes a visit to the Taj Mahal, one of the Seven Wonders of the World. The chance to propose to the love of your life at a location like that doesn't come around very often. I decided to speed things up a bit. After discussing it with close friends, I bought an engagement ring. As I was prepping for the trip, I realized that I had a bit of a problem. Because I was a foreign national in the U.S., I would be breaking the law if I traveled across the border without declaring the ring. Of course, declaring it would have ruined the surprise. Fernando Pica, soon to be the best man at my wedding, came up with the idea of having a replica made from white gold and glass. This was a great idea, allowing me to "smuggle" the fake ring without ruining the surprise.

As it turns out, Jenn almost found the ring on the plane from New York to New Delhi. I had hidden it in my wallet, thinking it would stay in my pocket for the three days until we reached the Taj Mahal. Four hours into the fourteen-hour flight, we decided it was cocktail time, so I absentmindedly handed Jenn my wallet, as we have done many times in our travels. She asked me what the bump in the outside of the wallet was, but thankfully the flight attendant had just asked for a credit card, and I was off the hook. Jenn says that my face blanched white at that moment, and she now understands why. I was preparing to get down on one knee in the aisle of that Delta Air Lines 777 and propose. She let it go—thankfully—but part of me is convinced to this day that it tipped her off as to what was to come.

After a night in New Delhi, the second day of our two-week trip was scheduled for Agra. We were traveling with friends with whom I had gone to Columbia and who were helping to build Lime, who eventually would be in my wedding party. You can't park your car close to the Taj, because local authorities want to minimize any pollution nearby, so our guide parked the van about a mile away, and the six of us piled into an electric rickshaw. I had my wheelchair with me because the sites are all a great distance apart from each other. As we approached the grounds, we came to a gate. Well, it's probably not right to call it a gate; it was more like an ornate archway in a mammoth building that you walk through to get to the Taj Mahal buildings themselves. We walked in, and the tour guide started giving us a brief explanation of the background of the site. I was sitting there with the ring loose in my left breast pocket, thinking, *Okay, when is the right time to do this?* I had never been to the Taj Mahal before, so I had no idea about timing and location. Everyone in our party knew what I was about to do, except Jenn.

Our tour guide pulled the six of us away from the flow of visitors and started telling us a story about why the Taj was built, that it was the ultimate monument to love. The Taj is perhaps the greatest exemplar of Mughal architecture in the world, and was commissioned by Mughal emperor Shah Jahan as a mausoleum for his wife Mumtaz Mahal, a Persian princess who died giving birth to their fourteenth child. The Taj illustrates the love story as it was documented by the Imperial Court at the time. The principal mausoleum was completed in 1643 and the surrounding buildings and garden were finished about five years later.

This was the narrative I was counting on to set the stage for the proposal. I assumed the guide would tell this story. I took that as a sign, thinking, *Okay, time to act.* I stood up from my wheelchair—my friends knew this was coming, so they were ready for it—but Jenn looked puzzled and asked, "Why are you standing up?" I asked Jenn to remove her sunglasses, and I did the same. "Wait, why? Why? Why?" she asked excitedly. Suddenly I dropped to one knee and said, "Jenn, please help me build a monument to love together. Let's make this Wonder look small. Will you marry me?"

Jenn hugged me, spun around in circles, and began to cry—I am pretty sure with joy. I remember asking, "Is that a yes?" and being thrilled at the prospect of building a life together. In minutes, we had a hundred people around us. Apparently, we had put on quite a show. There were two factors at play. One, you've got a well-dressed guy in a wheelchair proposing to a woman, and the woman is delighted. Two, you've got the idea of a "love marriage," versus the customary arranged marriage. Our tour guide was flabbergasted. He told us that he had been doing this for eighteen years and that this was the first proposal he had ever witnessed at the Taj Mahal. Which was shocking. I would have expected that it would happen every day. As a result, people stopped us the entire day long, taking our picture.

Engagement aside, the whole trip was like that. We were an oddity and a curiosity. It was like being on a great vacation and also onstage at the same time, with several surreal moments. The funny thing was that when we got back and Jenn told people about getting engaged at the Taj Mahal, they would comment, "Oh, the hotel over in Atlantic City? That's so romantic."

We take our progress in disability for granted in Western society because it's become somewhat integrated into most things that we do. Not the case in India at that time. We had some experiences over there that were mind-blowing, just very raw. These things don't happen in North America or Europe. In India, people with disabilities are not enjoying most of the gains made in the last three decades in the West. At least, they weren't at that time. They were mainly on the street. So when someone like me comes along, people in service positions have no idea what to do.

The last place we went before Shantha's nuptials was Udaipur, a city in Rajasthan known for its incredible palaces. From there we had to fly to Bangalore to get to the wedding. That was an interesting experience. I was using a wheelchair, and they didn't want to let me board the plane, saying my safety could not be guaranteed. Their approach was simple: to board the aircraft, I must waive all my legal rights. It was shocking. Had I been more of an activist, I would have fought it. That was an excellent example of knowing when to pick your battles. With disability, if you try to fight every little battle, you're going to chase your tail to eternity. I was pissed; I was angry that these idiots were trying to trample on my rights—only because they did not know any other way. I had bought a ticket to get on this airplane, they were letting everybody else board it, but I had to sign a waiver. I think it was my friend Danny who said, "This isn't the kind of battle you want to fight." It was a wake-up call for me that there are still fundamental issues in countries outside of North America and Europe that need addressing. If that had happened in the U.S., I would have owned the airline within two years.

The wedding was a beautiful affair. Just awe-inspiring. Afterwards, we took a train from Mysore to Bangalore for our flight back to Delhi. At the airport, we didn't have much time to spare. When we got to the Kingfisher Airlines counter, the woman instinctively started talking to Jenn, ignoring me in my wheelchair. Indicating me, she said, "I'm going to need to hold on to his passport." They wanted to take me away with my passport and have me examined by a doctor. Jenn started explaining about CP, and at that point, I cut it off. I said, "I'm either getting on this airplane or calling the police. It's up to you." Jenn said, "You're infringing on his rights. He's not sick; he's not ill." That woman had probably never dealt with this before.

I used to get fired up about this kind of thing all the time. I would say, "No, I'm a customer, do what you do for every other customer." I would get aggressive; I would yell and swear. If you catch me in the wrong mood, I'll regress to that approach today. But I had to learn that it's very rarely malice on the part of the person I'm dealing with; it's ignorance. Nowadays I go into teaching mode. I calmly explain what they're doing wrong. If they still don't get it, I use some colorful language, but I keep my cool.

These kinds of things don't happen just in places like India; they happen all over the place. I run into similar situations with taxi drivers, for example, right here in North America. The way we dealt with it in the past was to put up a fight, verbally. The way we need to deal with it in the future is to demand change as a customer. Take the situation with Kingfisher Airlines. While the airline was known for high-touch customer service, they failed horribly when it came to dealing with disability. Who knows, per-haps Kingfisher's poor management lay at the root of their lack of process and sophistication. After an ill-timed purchase of a no-frills airline, Kingfisher couldn't handle its expanded empire. It consistently lost money and failed to master the complexity of the airline business, accumulating losses of over US$1 billion. India's Directorate General of Civil Aviation grounded Kingfisher for good in 2012. Well-run companies tend to be better on disability issues because they perform better in general.

When experiences like Kingfisher occur, I could do one of two things as a person with disabilities. I had the choice of giving into my anger, getting litigious, and lodging complaints. Or, I could calmly sit down with management and say, "Look, here's your business opportunity, here's how you handled this wrong, here's how you can change it." It has taken time, but my mindset has evolved from getting angry to being constructive. It's difficult to remain frosty-headed and sharp when three-quarters of your experiences as a customer are at best mediocre and at worst outright insulting and discriminatory.

Incidents like this make you realize that social change is not some monolithic blanket that you peel back. It's an organizational process that involves real people, that involves institutions changing what they do on a day-to-day basis. That takes a relentless and consistent effort based on proven business strategy. It's something that you must actively manage within an organization. It's portrayed much differently in the media, partly because very gradual, day-to-day social change is not sexy. It doesn't pull at the heartstrings. Strategy is effective but boring.

If you were coming from another planet, watching the history of the Earth on television, you would think civil rights occurred because somebody named Martin Luther King Jr. crossed a bridge. That was a trigger, but ultimately civil rights came into being because millions of people demanded that society and its institutions make it happen. The same will hold true for disability in the next five years.

Social change occurs when institutions change how they do things. And institutions rarely change without outside influence and pressure. It's easy to show a clip of a group of young people walking across a bridge, but they are not the real heroes, even though that's what the media and political actors celebrate. The reality is, it's not that clean. Getting it done is a dirty process. It takes time and iteration and hard work. When 1.3 billion people start to demand what they need from institutions, that changes the game. That changes everything. But it doesn't happen in a speech or a walk. It takes a decade of consumer interaction to alter society. We're on our way to that goal.

What finally got things moving at the Kingfisher Airlines counter was that Jenn stopped talking. She has learned that clamming up makes people deal with me, which is good because then they quickly realize that I'm with it. I'm calm, I'm reasonable, and in this case I said something along the lines of "Look, here's the deal. I have an airplane to catch in thirty-five minutes; you need to figure out what you want to do. We need to be on that plane because we must be back in New York tomorrow. So figure out what you're going to do, come back to me and give me a solution. I think you have about three minutes to figure it out before I miss my plane." Pretty quickly we had four people whisk us through the airport to catch our flight.

CHAPTER TWENTY

RITES OF PASSAGE:
FROM FIANCÉ TO FATHERHOOD

J enn and I got married on December 6, 2008, a little over two years after we first met. Unfortunately, Jenn's dad passed away suddenly, three months before the wedding. Jenn was about to start her new job with Avon Products, and I was six months into my start-up, now The Return on Disability Group. While Lime would continue its narrow focus on recruiting students on campus, The Return on Disability Group would advise companies across their business to build value. The big win for most firms is revenue growth, and Return on Disability was focused on building value across the firm—not just talent.

Jenn's father passed, the market imploded, Jenn embarked on a new career, I started a new business in the worst recession since the Great Depression . . . there was just a little bit going on at that point in our lives. We chose to have a destination wedding because we figured it would be too tricky to pick between

Toronto and New York. NYC would probably be too expensive for what we wanted to do in any case. So we got married at the Fairmont Royal Pavilion in Barbados. It was a toss-up between the Fairmont and Sandy Lane, which is where Tiger Woods got married. I wanted Sandy Lane, Jenn wanted Fairmont; Jenn made the right choice.

When Jenn's father passed away, the wedding invitations had just gone out. The wedding and her dad's death overlapped in a way that was less than ideal, but there were some humorous moments, believe it or not. At her dad's wake, around two in the afternoon, Jenn's cell phone rang. It was the bridal shop letting her know that her gown had arrived a few weeks early. There we were, standing in a quiet crowd of people paying their respects to her father, and Jenn's getting a call from a delightfully happy woman about her beautiful new wedding dress. Jenn said, "I'm sorry I have to call you back, I'm . . . I'm at my father's wake," and hung up. She started crying, and I walked her outside. Once we were alone, I tried to lighten the mood. "Come on Jenn," I said, "this has to make you laugh. You can't write this stuff." Looking at me, she caught the giggles. We had a cathartic laugh and got through that tough time, and went down to get married in Barbados in the company of some wonderful people.

I had been to Barbados a few times as a kid; it was my fifth or sixth time down there. Jenn and I been once together to scout it out, and now we're in love with the place. Now when we land in Barbados, we feel like we're home.

We had sixty of our closest friends and relatives join us for what turned out to be an incredible week. A bunch of events were scheduled—a sunset sail, the rehearsal dinner and the wedding, on the beach, right before Christmas—the perfect time to be in Barbados. The energy in the room that night was electric. It was a three-day trip for the people who came.

We had the honeymoon in Fiji—from one paradise to another.

Once in Fiji, we collapsed for two weeks. I think we slept the whole first day. We were just exhausted. Our hotel was on a private island about a mile in diameter. There were these gorgeous huts and a pool on top of a cliff overlooking the ocean. Just spectacular, right? And somehow—I still don't know how this happened—when I was getting off the boat onto the dock of the resort, I sprained my ankle. So I was having trouble walking that week. Jenn was piggybacking me everywhere. When she carried me to dinner, the owner of the hotel came over and asked if there was anything he could do to make our stay more comfortable. I said, "You wouldn't have a wheelchair here, would you?"

He said, "No, but you know what? I'll order one for you."

When it came, two days later, he got on a boat, went over to the mainland, and brought it back himself. In the meantime, he gave us a number to call whenever we needed to go somewhere. We would call, and a few minutes later three big Fijian guys would arrive and carry me wherever we wanted. It was classic.

For every unpleasant experience I have had, there are probably twenty examples of people adapting their service for me. To my way of thinking, it has less to do with disability and more to do with what the customer wants. You certainly wouldn't expect a wheelchair to show up within forty-eight hours on a remote Fijian island. So it's nice when something like that happens. And that wheelchair will be there for the next guest that wants it. The change that was made to benefit me has the potential to improve the experience for any guest. That's something that you can apply to any situation.

Let me give you an example. I travel a lot for business, and since I have CP I tend to wind up staying in hotel rooms with accessible bathrooms, even though that's not generally something I need. It's just one of those trivial things hotels do to try and make their lawyers happy. These are nicer hotels, so it's always shocking to find that my bathroom is invariably among the ugliest you will ever see in your life. Now, according to so-called universal design, these bathrooms are perfect. But if a disability advocate tried talking a hotel chain into putting these bathrooms into all their suites, they would be laughed out of the room on the basis of aesthetics alone, let alone price. Yes, they meet all the functional needs required for some people with disabilities, but they fail to meet my needs as a customer. That's because universal design is a misnomer. It's an architectural concept that deals with design specific to disability. What it should mean is that you are designing things for widespread use that also work for people with disabilities. If you take a car and make it easier to drive for a guy with very little arm strength, for example, you've just made the car easier for everybody to drive. That concept applies everywhere.

One summer, we rented a house on Fire Island that we would go to on the weekends. Fire Island is a barrier island a few miles off the south coast of Long Island, about an hour away from New York City. In August 2009, at the end of that summer, we organically decided that maybe we should start thinking about having a child.

That November, Jenn had to go to China for a two-week work trip to visit manufacturers. Jenn was feeling "a little off" when she departed for China. After a week of feeling the same way, her intuition led her to acquire a pregnancy test. She was in Hong Kong at the time. Jenn knew that when she embarked on the next leg of her trip, to mainland China, she would be visiting factories in areas where little English is spoken, and getting a test would have been more of an unknown. She bought the test, and, well, a positive result was the outcome. It was a leap for both of us that we were apart at that life changing moment. Jenn remembers the moment this way:

So the next minute, here I was looking at this stick in a bathroom at the Mandarin Oriental in Hong Kong, and it said I was pregnant. I couldn't believe it. I felt like I couldn't breathe for a second, and I was crying. I had every emotion run through me all at once . . . joy, fear, confusion, more fear, and sadness because Rich wasn't there. I wanted so much for Rich to be there to share this moment. Then I had to focus on keeping a poker face and finish the meeting I was having with an Avon jewelry manufacturer, reacting appropriately to the assortment of semi-precious stones he was showing me—having just found out that I was pregnant one minute earlier.

Finally the meeting ended and I ran up to my hotel room to contact Rich, as I had another meeting in an hour. I was hyperventilating. I IMed Rich, hoping he would be awake, as it was about 11 p.m. in New York at that point. When he called me, I blurted out the news that I was pregnant, and we laughed, and I think he even cried a little. It's amazing, because even though I couldn't see him (this was before I used Skype), I could see his face in my mind. He had his "game on!" face, while I'll admit that I was totally overwhelmed. The trip lasted another week or so, and that sixteen-hour flight home was the longest of my life. I had a million thoughts going through my head and every emotion. I remember arriving at our apartment, bleary-eyed, and Rich opened the door with this huge smile and open arms. Rich has this way of making everything in the world seem possible, and a piece of cake at that. In that moment of seeing him, all my fears subsided, and the excitement began.

Jenn had a feeling that it was a boy right from the beginning—as a data guy, I've learned to trust her gut, as it tends to be right. She came home one day and said, "I have the perfect name." When I asked what it was, she said, "Maverick." I thought for a minute and said, "That's a little aggressive, isn't it?" But then she explained that, aside from the fact that we both love the movie *Top Gun*, "maverick" means someone who changes the rules. I was blown away. I thought it was brilliant. So it stuck. The best names are not the ones with instant appeal—they are the ones that you come around to, just like Lime.

Not long after we chose the baby's name, we went sailing. It was the first time we had ever sailed alone together, and Jenn was six months pregnant. Jenn's family was a little nervous about us chartering a boat and going off into the middle of the Caribbean Sea, but it was one of our last hurrahs before the baby came. I joke that I'm more stable on a boat than on land, and I was eager to show Jenn the ropes. Now, living on a boat for a week is a big change if you've never done it before. It's tight quarters. You're living right on top of each other. Jenn used to get nervous with change, whereas I incite change; I seek it out. It's the same thing with sailing. Jenn just needed to do it.

I have always felt that immersion is the best and the quickest way to learn something. But immersion experiences can be uncomfortable if you're not used to them. At the beginning of the trip, I said, "Look, here's what's going to happen. I'm going to use words that you don't understand. I'm going to tell you to do things and you're going to think I'm speaking a different language altogether. Don't worry about it; you'll get it. Take your time and just go with it." And she did. It can be tough to get accustomed to at first, but Jenn got it very quickly, and now she's a sailor. She has developed a love for sailing and can handle a boat.

Maverick first made his presence known on that trip. I was glad that it happened on a sailing voyage. In Trellis Bay, in the British Virgin Islands, Jenn jumped off the back of the boat for a swim. She says that when she hit the water, her belly felt exceptionally light and buoyant. Then she felt movement for the first time, like Maverick was awakened—right there in the waters of the Caribbean Sea. Sea legs in utero—atta boy!

The anticipation of becoming a father raises fears and doubts in the mind of every man, and I was no exception. Three things in my life have caused me to worry about whether I could do them: moving to New York City, starting a business, and managing an infant. I fully intended to be a very active dad and had to figure out how. It was all about how we were going to manage it with CP. I could work my head around what picking him up and feeding him looked like and pretty much everything else . . . except for the crib. I wanted to be able to put my son in a crib and reach over and pick him up if I needed to. And I wanted to be able to do it on my knees. My balance on my knees is perfect, while my balance on my feet would later be described by seven-year-old Maverick as "wobbly."

We couldn't find an off-the-shelf crib that would work for me. I thought about kneeling on a chair and picking Maverick up that way, or sawing the legs off an existing product—but those options were less than optimal. The obvious answer, in my mind, was a crib with a door built into the side. Our first searches for this specific feature turned up options that resembled either a birdcage or a pigpen, prompting amusing thoughts of Maverick's future on a farm or in therapy—or both.

After a frustrating search, my dad and I ended up designing a crib with a door that met Jenn's and my aesthetic desires as well as functional requirements. The next challenge was that we couldn't get anybody to build it. Furniture designed for kids is probably one of the most regulated industries in the world. People will not deviate at all from regulations because of the potential liability. We were about three or four months into the pregnancy, wondering, *How are we going to do this with the crib?*

It turns out that someone had been making a crib precisely like the one I had imagined. It's called BabeeTenda, and it has a double door in the slide slats with a childproof opening mechanism. It's one of the best-built cribs you've ever seen in your life. The Hummer of cribs. Big too. Kind of like a king-sized bed for a baby. Lucky kid, eh?

The first time I picked Maverick up, I was terrified. I had this tiny human in my arms, and I'm thinking, *Okay, Rich, protect the football* . . . I wanted to be able to do all the things that a dad does, and the truth is you have to make it up as you go along. It was a design-on-the-fly kind of mindset. Swaddle blankets became carriers. If I had to move Maverick, I always had a blanket or a sleep sack to pick him up with. That way I could just stick him in his stroller in the blanket and roll him to the next destination. I didn't have to carry him the way most people do, nor would that approach have been as safe.

By opening the range of possible solution sets, and thinking ahead, Jenn and I faced the same uncertainties that all new parents face—with a twist. The solutions we came up with were always straightforward and low-cost. I was amazed how well they worked. But you don't know they are going to work until you are in the moment. The big learning for me was: don't stress about the unknown details; you'll figure it out when you get there. Action building strategy, not the other way around.

Speaking of "in the moment," Maverick's birth itself was fantastic. Three days beforehand, I was at a board meeting in

Washington. I had the hotel keep a car on standby to drive me to New York in case she went into labor. Unusually, I kept my mobile phone on. I have never really embraced mobile communication; with CP, mobile is not easy. Luckily, it wasn't necessary; I made my train back to Manhattan in plenty of time for the birth.

On what turned out to be Maverick's birthday, I was up early to catch a train to Purchase, New York, to meet with the CMO of Pepsi Beverages. As I was set to head out the door, Jenn mentioned that something didn't "feel right." She was due in a week, and we knew to be additionally cautious. She called our doctor, and as a precaution we went into the hospital.

"Go bag" in tow, Jenn was given some tests upon arrival at New York-Presbyterian Weill Cornell Medical Center, a quick cab ride up the FDR Drive from our downtown John Street apartment. A doctor came in soon after, looked at me, and quietly asked, "Are you ready to be a father today?" She said she would "get the ball rolling" and be right back.

Jenn looked at me and asked, "Wait . . . what did she just say?"

I smiled. "They're going to induce labor. Today is the day, Mommy."

If you have not been through childbirth as a father, it is—by far—the easier of the two team roles. I am in abject awe of the process and the outcome. My day consisted of taking Jenn's mind off the contractions and staying out of the way as much as possible. I tried to make Jenn's life as easy as possible for as long as possible, while she brought another life into the world. All you dads out there, you know what I mean.

I'm not squeamish, and I consider myself an uber-geek, so watching Maverick's birth from the front row blew my mind. About eleven hours after we arrived at the hospital, a new face was testing his new lungs. Wow. What an amazing process to watch unfold. As the doctors finished up the birthing process with Jenn, they handed me this bundle that fit nicely onto my lap. Again, wow. With Maverick in her arms, Jenn looked just radiant. It was one of the happiest moments in both our lives.

Before the induction, the hospital staff let me know that the child might not respond to my voice right away, as babies tend to gravitate to Mom's voice thanks to in-utero vibrations. I remember that after he was born, the nurse put Maverick under a light and asked me to "spend the next twenty-five minutes slapping his feet with your hand and talking to him to keep him crying and awake." I figured, *Okay, I can do that*. No sooner did I open my mouth than Maverick swiveled his little head toward me. My voice was so completely different from every other voice he had heard while in the womb. He knew right away what that was. "Don't stop talking," they said, "we're going to make sure that he's reacting to the things that he's supposed to be reacting to." I spent the first twenty-five minutes of Maverick's life giving him an introductory lecture on monetary policy. I was talking about money supply, debt-to-GDP ratios, and how we were going through unprecedented economic times . . . it was the first thing that came into my head. As I said, uber-geek.

The day we left the hospital was fun for me. I now had this new identity as a dad, and a dad with a visible disability at that. Most people who saw us had no clue how to react to that—except that it certainly appeared that they thought it was impressive. Walking into the hospital that morning, pushing an empty baby carriage, was surreal. I was doing what every dad before me had done, and every dad after me will do, yet you would think I'd just walked off the Red Sox to win the World Series. Guys I'd never met were high-fiving me. Nurses were smiling. Huh? Then it dawned on me—this doesn't happen a lot. Society's expectation of people with visible disabilities does not include "parent." Add on the fact that I at least appeared to know what I was doing—we were over-prepared—and I now realize how much of a paradox I was at that moment from a perception point of view. We loaded the little guy into a yellow cab and went home as a family.

We were living in the financial district, renting a unit in a condo building. Well before our lease expired, the owner decided to sell our apartment and gave us sixty days' notice. So we had to go looking for apartments back on the Upper West Side, where we'd lived together just before we got engaged, but now with a two-month-old baby. That was interesting. Jenn would push me in the wheelchair, and I would push the stroller. We called it "the love train." You can picture this train moving up Amsterdam Avenue on the Upper West Side and people going, "What is that?" Maverick appeared to enjoy it. Movement lulls all babies. Later, he loved going on my scooter. As soon as he could sit up on his own, we would put Maverick in the basket with his little legs dangling through the holes. We would drive around the Upper West Side, Central Park, and out by the Hudson River with this six-month-old kid sitting in the scooter basket, making baby eyes at everyone who walked by.

For a long time now, whenever Maverick builds a structure, he puts ramps on it so that my scooter can access it. Not like we ever told him to do it. He is almost eight now, and it wasn't until we took him on a trip to Barbados when he was just under five that he discovered disability. He and Jenn went into an accessible hotel bathroom, and Maverick asked, "Why is this bathroom so big?"

"It's a bathroom for people with disabilities," Jenn told him.

"What's disability?" he asked.

"Well, it's when people do things a little differently," Jenn explained, "you know, like maybe walk a little differently."

"Oh, like Daddy," he reasoned.

"Yeah, like Daddy. You know, a little wobbly, just a bit different." And that was that. That was the first instance disability came up.

THREE

GETTING A
RETURN ON
DIFFERENT

CHAPTER TWENTY-ONE
A MARKET THE SIZE OF CHINA

After I left Merrill in March 2008, I started The Return on Disability Group the following Monday. It's a step that, if I had been solely motivated by money, I should not have taken. If I was purely rational, I would have found an opportunity in any space other than this one. The probability of commercial success in disability—at that moment especially—was low. There was a long list of failures in the space that had come before me, and there were many efforts currently under way in the space that were on their way to failure. I'm convinced that I'm a fool. But as a trader, you do the math and see this market of 1.3 billion people worldwide—a market the size of China—and you think, *Even a tiny probability of success is going to outweigh the downside*. When friends and family of PWD are included, disability touches 53 percent of consumers. The opposite of niche. The opportunity is huge.

Lime was an easy way to test that. While I had a good job, I figured I would test it out, no risk, and see if it worked. Lime worked well. It was proof for me that the market was ready to be engaged—both from the point of view of engaging people with disabilities and engaging corporations. I realized that if this were done in a professional way that met expectations and produced a certain level of quality, companies would buy, and the market would engage. I didn't know the extent to which the market would respond. It turns out I underestimated a little bit; it happened quicker than I thought—I was nervous, but the math was right all along.

Very few people think that way. The math also said that it was going to be five years of almost no response. It said that I was going to struggle alone for a long time, until the market came to me. Both turned out to be true. Not a lot of people are willing to sink ten years of their lives into an endeavor with less than a 1 percent chance of success, especially a 1 percent chance of success in an enormous marketplace littered with failures. Failure after failure after failure. You've got Disaboom, a website launched in 2007 dedicated to disability that raised $24 million in external capital and lost every dime. Disaboom attempted to be a "one-stop shop" for people with disabilities. Disabled sports. Disabled movies. Disabled fashion. Disabled blah blah blah. Too much disability sunk it. Some magazines tried to focus on this market, some of which lost $25 million in capital, never to see a red cent come back. People had been trying to do disability since the 1980s and losing their shirts in the process.

Since I had become something of a subject matter expert on disability and had tasted success with Lime, I figured that I had a better chance than most. I want to give some credit to Charlie Hammerman. His father was the one who had convinced me to join Merrill Lynch, and Charlie had been one of my biggest champions in my early career at Merrill. Charlie was a director in equity capital markets who had helped set disability strategy for the firm. I worked with him on the firm's disability employee resource group (ERG). Charlie was one of the leading advocates around disability in the business world at the time. He still is. His advocacy is born out of a passion for his daughter, who has CP and is now regularly kicking ass on her own terms as a CrossFit coach.

During my career at Merrill, Charlie and I were talking about building an investment fund around disability. I had been running away from disability my entire career, and Charlie got me to think about it differently. Up until that point in the business world, disability had been discussed in a sociopolitical context that was tied not to profit but to a moral imperative. Even my early conversations with Charlie were around that. We understood the need to drive disability from a business perspective, but we were having the "why" conversation as opposed to the "how." It was clear to me that the why was easy to understand but not the how.

I commend Charlie for his leadership and the important work he's done since leaving Merrill. He chose a different path than I did, but he's making an impact. He helped create the Burton Blatt Institute at Syracuse University to advance civic, economic, and social participation of persons with disabilities in a global society. Then, in 2007, he started the Disability Opportunity Fund "to provide technical and financial services to individuals and organizations serving the disability market throughout the United States, with a focus on affordable housing, schools, and vocational training centers." The fund is the first CDFI created for the disabled community.

The idea of disability being part of business has been around for over thirty years. It is not a new concept, but no one had quantified it. No one had built a measurement model to act in a repeatable way to build value. No one had treated it as a market. That was something new to both companies and investors. So I started putting numbers around it, discovering what it looked like as a market—its size, spending power, and other metrics that influence valuation.

Institutional investors are not used to hearing about valuation relating to socially responsible investing, or "impact investing," as it is increasingly known. Most impact investing is driven by a set of policy goals unrelated to returns. Institutional fund managers have a fiduciary duty to get the best returns that they can for their clients—clients that are often pensioners. There is no bigger fiduciary mandate than that which concerns pensioners. They get protected in unbelievable ways, as they should.

If pension fund CIOs don't deliver gains of 7 or 8 percent per year, in ten years they are going to be billions of dollars short when people retire, and pensions will get cut, or the public purse will make up for the shortfall. So, when they look at socially responsible investing (SRI) and see 1 percent, 2 percent, maybe 5 percent—returns that do not meet expectations—you can't blame them for not getting excited. And when they see the methodology, that company x has a system for washing water after they use it, for example, they think, *What does that have to do with maximizing returns?* The social goal may be clear, but the investment goal is not.

Impact investing can be a difficult conversation to have with institutional investors because they take their fiduciary responsibilities very seriously. Still, quite a few large-fund managers have been handed mandates for SRI investing. A good example is the Norwegian sovereign wealth fund, a fund of almost a trillion dollars. Every dollar invested must have an environmental, social, and governance component. The Norwegian fund has the biggest mandate I know of, but these mandates exist everywhere. They are generally environmentally focused and have at best a tangential connection to shareholder value. No guns, no coal, no oil, no gas. It's a nice idea to some. But it's not linked to making money.

Most investment funds' customer bases consist of large institutional investors. What does the customer demand? Performance.

They have a benchmark that they must meet every year to be able to pay their beneficiaries when they retire. That's around 7 or 8 percent. It's awfully difficult to meet that benchmark, especially in today's environment of low interest rates. And now you're coming in and saying, "Hey, I also want you to invest here. You're going to underperform, but do it anyway." That's silly. It puts the investor in conflict with their main goals. Companies exist for one reason and one reason only: to build value for shareholders. Anything else is just noise. So a lot of investors are pushing back on it. They're saying, "I can't do that. I'm going to put myself in legal jeopardy and fail to maximize financial returns."

The impact investing/shareholder value conundrum is something that had been rattling around in the back of my mind for years. When we got Lime up and running, I started thinking more and more about how disability relates to business. Lime was a recruiting process that was certainly needed. It essentially delivered on a subset of what would become the Return on Disability model. Still, it didn't provide the complete answer. As I did my research, I started to develop the macro argument for Return on Disability. I began to understand that hiring and recruiting and jobs were small pieces of the puzzle. I saw a bigger opportunity in serving the customer and delivering an experience that would cause them to shift their spend to a brand that did disability well.

I understood intuitively that the way to get the customer to vote with their wallet would be through developing products and customer experiences that delighted not only customers with disabilities but the core customer as well. That concept was easy to understand for me. What was missing was the mechanism for getting large organizations to build that into their everyday processes. How do you get a multinational with three hundred thousand employees and operations in just about every country in the world to take this concept and make it real, every day? Because at the end of the day, building value is about helping an organization build more and better transactions: products and experiences in exchange for money. It's not about policy; it's not about regulation or supporting a charity. It's about increasing the quantity and quality of transactions with customers and the factors of production—including employees.

The light bulb went on. It dawned on me that we needed to find a way to convince corporations to change behavior that would increase the value of the billions of transactions that happen every day as they touch the disability market. If you think about it, there are a lot of things upstream of a monetary transaction. You have to see ads, pick products off shelves, read the ingredients, hear about the company in the news, visit their sales outlet, their website, or talk to their call center employees. Just to name a few. Companies come into your life in many little ways, and each time there is a transaction: you learn something, you feel something, and it's either positive or negative. That positive or negative feeling influences your likelihood to engage in or increase the size of a purchase.

I ultimately concluded that the socioeconomic needs of people with disabilities are aligned with the requirements of investors to maximize returns. I see no reason why we can't unlock social value in this marketplace, change corporate behavior, and maximize returns. While many indices in the impact investing sector focus on drivers that are wholly unrelated to shareholder value, with RoD, shareholder value is the primary driver. As Return on Disability gains momentum, more companies will want to attract the capital that invests in the index. To achieve that, they must attract more people with disabilities as both customers and sources of talent.

My first step in setting up the measurement model was to take disability out of the realm of the theoretical. I started with how a company touches a person with a disability (and/or their friends and family). It doesn't get much more transactional than touch, so

I came to call those transactions "touchpoints." Whether you're picking up a product in a retail environment or applying for a job, you have to touch something or contact someone. It's a very intimate thing; it's a very individual conversation.

The wonderful thing was that there were plenty of models out there in other markets that we could look at. High-quality brands measure customer impact day in, day out. So all we had to do was take this good business practice that they were already comfortable with and put a disability twist on it to serve that particular market need. That was something brand managers understood. Something that product developers understood. Something that recruiters understood.

Until that point—and this hasn't changed *at all* with organizations other than The Return on Disability Group—people had been presenting companies and managers with a charity or policy message, not a business message. I was designing a matrix comprised of these touchpoints, intersected by a formula for measuring the impact of activities taken by companies toward those touchpoints. My algorithm then resulted in a measure of each company's positive impact on disability factors.

Each of these touchpoints is a basic business process. They're not hard to get right. But because companies are so afraid of putting a foot wrong in an area that very few people understand, they get all twisted up in their knickers, things get complicated, and the risk goes up.

These actions are directly linked to one (or both) of two possible results: higher revenue and/or lower cost. If an action couldn't achieve one (or both) of these fundamental building blocks of value, it was not a compelling impetus for change. This is critical to Return on Disability's success. For companies to change behavior, things must be easy to do. The beauty of Lime was that all they had to do was show up and hire people. There was no risk. They showed up; they got great people. Who wouldn't do that?

In December 2007, I was sitting on the trading floor with this touchpoint concept in my head. It was during the dead days right before Christmas, when everything is quiet. India was all ready to go; I had the ring for Jenn, I had everything set. It was about eight o'clock in the morning, and I said to myself, *Okay, I'm going to spend the day putting this down on paper.* Which is a key step for any entrepreneur. I spent the day writing out every possible disability-related touchpoint that I could come up with that had to do with a corporation. Products, signage, packaging, job application forms, parking lots, front door, store, counter, hallways, lighting . . . everything that would impact your experience as a customer or as a job candidate. Every tiny, minute way that a customer or a candidate could be touched by the company, whether they were at company headquarters, in a store, or sitting in their living room.

I came up with 302 touchpoints over two days. Examples included on-brand imagery, embedded features that enhance customer experience, and the number of actual hires made relative to the company's total workforce. I made sure that these were strictly customer and candidate touchpoints, not employee touchpoints. That was critical. If I had to get inside the company to measure something, how the hell was I going to do that? To be honest with you, I didn't know what I had at that point. I just wanted to get it on paper, file it away, and start thinking about what to do with it. I went to lunch, came back to the desk, and sat down, wondering what I was going to call this thing. I wanted a value-added name, something that already registered as a financial term. I was thinking in terms of acronyms. I started to do a search for designations and measurements—ROI, EBITDA, EPS, EVA—trying to get my head around, okay, what does the financial world use to identify key measurements? EVA (economic value added) stuck with me because while EVA is a number, you have to go through an extensive evaluation process to get a meaningful EVA. I wanted the name to have some real-world weight. I wanted it to be robust and chunky, because I knew that it had to speak to the business model.

At that point, I had no clue what I was eventually going to ask companies to sign on for. I knew it involved a transfer of knowledge, guiding them through to the goal of attracting the disability market—what to do, how to do it, and how to measure success. But I didn't know what that looked like from an engagement or relationship point of view. I had some idea, but until you get in there with the client, you don't know what you're going to find.

I probably had a hundred acronyms up on my screen at one point. That was what the market accepted as real, so that's the direction I went. And then it came to me. I was looking at ROI; I was looking at disability. I said, *Yikes, what if it's as simple as "Return on Disability"?* I called Jenn right away and said, "I got it. I got it! The name is Return on Disability!" She loved it.

"I remember that conversation," Jenn recalls. "Rich's voice gets fast and high-pitched when he's really excited about a work breakthrough, and when he called that day, I knew immediately he had some really good news."

I was excited because I wanted something that looked, felt, and tasted like any other financial metric. I knew what I was looking for . . . I just didn't know what I was looking for—if you get my meaning. Once I had it, there was no deliberation. It was just "That's it! That's it!" Twenty minutes after I came up with the name, I had the URL. That was the day I decided to leave Merrill Lynch.

The naming process was quick, but that's typical for me. I always spend a lot of time quietly thinking before I do or say anything. Nobody knows what's going on inside except me. Then at some point I'll just say to myself, *Damn, I need to sit down and type this out.* I will just dump it all out. It won't be in any usable format typically—sometimes it's absolutely perfect, but that's rare—but when I'm sitting down to do that, all the work is already done, all the thinking is done, I'm at a point where I've thought about it for long enough and it's time to sit down and put pen to paper. (Or, as is usual in my case, build a spreadsheet model.)

Lime was my test to see if business was ready for a market-driven message. It was. It was hungry for that. Businesses can't wait to get away from the same old charity crap and get a return on investment. To make that happen, RoD had to be easy to understand, be low risk, and produce measurable results. With Return on Disability, everything we measure goes back to returns: how companies can create value by acting in disability. We had to show wins. It couldn't be this amorphous "Yeah, we ran an ad, and we don't quite know what results that produced."

What I'm doing now is breaking the mold of socially conscious investing (SRI). I'm saying that it's bullshit. You can't just invest in a company because they are nice. Nice doesn't pay the bills. I can't go to a widow and say, "Here's your pension money back with a 'nice' return. Go spend this 'nice' at your local grocery store." Nice doesn't work there. You must base these metrics on something real.

The good news is that real SRI exists. I have proven the concept of promoting social responsibility and serving a market while making money. Socially responsible investing no longer must revolve around doing the right thing rather than good returns. You don't have to do it because the government says you must. You can do it because it makes more money for shareholders.

A crucial point to make about the Return on Disability model: I didn't just need measurable results but a repeatable process. I needed to be able to measure a change in metrics important to shareholders in order to convince them to do it again and again and again. The successes in the disability marketplace at that point were one-offs. Some champion had stuck her neck out and said, "We're going to do this," and it was successful, but there was no repeatable strategy or process behind it, no setup for future success. If that person left the company, it was gone. And that was happening all over the place. It's still happening today. An individual leads most corporate successes. That individual walks away, and the methodology behind the successful process they led leaves with them.

The model I needed had to be repeatable, scalable, easy to understand, easy to replicate internally, and tracked over time. For me, that pointed to what's called quality function deployment. QFD is something I learned at the dinner table from my father, one of the leading North American experts on the subject. The broad strokes are: you create a plan, you find benchmarks, you execute the plan, you revisit that execution vis-à-vis the parameters, and you continuously improve upon it. This process is viewed through the lens of direct customer feedback—no proxies. If it does not come out of a customer's mouth, it is disregarded. The standard approach up to that point was that organizations would have disability experts come in and say, "Here's where you suck, go fix it," then walk away. They were not providing a concrete plan to attract and delight customers and employees. They were leaving it up to the company to do that, and of course the company, never having done it before in this space, often failed.

My challenge was to build a sustainable operation that would equip organizations with the assets companies need to execute on disability. RoD now performs the same enterprise-wide assessment for all companies. We evaluate a company's performance—independent of the company—on disability touchpoints across both internal (employee-facing) and external (customer-facing) touchpoints. These touchpoints are publicly observable things that range from packaging to job applications to the reception desk at HQ. We simply change the weightings of the variables depending on what kind of company it is. If it's a consumer-facing company, we weigh customer touchpoints more heavily because the consumer is going to drive revenue growth for those businesses.

In a market this size, PepsiCo's biggest opportunity isn't hiring a disability recruiter. It's serving the customer. They face 95 percent of consumers, 53 percent of whom are tied to disability in some way. If they can shift that 53 percent even a little bit from Coke to Pepsi, they are going to beat their earnings expectations. That's a conversation that excites business leaders. That's a conversation that executives want to have.

We have proven that creating a better customer experience for people with disabilities must be simultaneous with creating a better experience for the core customer. People with disabilities don't want a Pepsi for the disabled, they want a package that is easier to open, which in turn makes it easier to open for every consumer. PWD don't want "visually impaired glasses," but if Google Glass devices are designed in a way that improves the customer experience of those with a vision issue, they'll be early adopters.

Nowadays, any competent manager can execute on RoD recommendations and chart her progress. You don't need to have a personal passion for disability to understand and apply it. Great companies do this every day in all industries. Seventy-five percent of businesses have ignored disability because most people just don't know that the opportunity exists. When I'm speaking to an audience, and I ask, "What do you think disability is?" hands go up: "In a wheelchair"; "A white cane" . . . that's literally what they think disability is.

"Rich, you say disability is so big, but I don't see too many wheelchairs around." I get this comment all the time. When I explain that only 5 to 7 percent of individuals with disabilities use a wheelchair, a light bulb goes on, and they start to get it.

After sitting on boards and working with a wide variety of organizations in the disability space, I realize that I have a distinct perspective that very few people in this area, if any, have. In 2007 I realized that I had the opportunity to be *the* global expert in a market the size of China. That's what drove me. At this point, I'm still the only one doing it, but that will change. If I'm right, smart people will take the risk to leave Google, Goldman, and McKinsey to serve this market.

Historically, if you look at innovation, things tend to happen at the same time. It's a concept called *multiple discovery* in which separate groups come up with the same or similar ideas simultaneously. Examples of this include calculus in the seventeenth century, the discovery of oxygen in the eighteenth century, and the theory of evolution in the nineteenth century. The way I rationalize it is, if you don't see competition, you have put a foot wrong. Ideally, you want to see the competition that can't get it right. That's what we see now in disability, but eventually you will get someone that does get it right. I will never be the only player in this game. The head start that I got, which at the time was painful and, to be honest, extremely stressful both for my new family and me, has turned out to be a huge advantage. I also had the added benefit of the market damping risk during a recession. I was the only fool willing to take that chance at that time. Now I'm beyond the difficult days of building.

I spent the first two weeks of March 2008 training people on what I did at Merrill. After hours, I was building RoD. I put together the LLC and filed for a trademark. When I woke up on my last day at Merrill, I asked myself, once again, what the hell I was doing. *Am I a fool? I have a fantastic job; I work for a great company that pays me a lot of money—what am I doing?* But what I kept coming back to is that you never get these opportunities. *Ever.* A market the size of China? Forget about it. Three years earlier, I couldn't even have come up with that scenario. And I have a wild imagination. That's what drove me then, and it's what's driving me now. The opportunity is enormous.

While I was nervous about going out on my own, I was confident that I would be successful. I guess I should stop there and say that up until that point, the most prominent fear in life that I still had not confronted was starting my own business. It was also something that I desperately wanted to do. So, by opening that door, I was overcoming my biggest fear. Hanging my shingle out was a big deal for me. I had this mental picture I carried around with me at the time of a wooden shingle with "Rich" on it hanging off a doorknob. When I did it, it felt great. It felt awesome.

Another thing is going out on my own meant that I had a shot at doing something great. You can be comfortable if you do well, but unless you're the founder it's very difficult to chart the course, even if you're CEO. I knew that I had to do this to build something great. You want to do something impactful, something that will change the world. And the way that I knew how to do that was through business.

Now, I'm talking about wealth, I'm talking about making money, and a lot of people will read this wealth and success stuff and say, *Geez, this guy is a frigging mercenary.* And it's true that I was as far removed from "nice to do" as I could get. That is 100 percent intentional. I didn't want to touch "nice to do" with a ten-foot pole. That was the opposite of what I wanted. But keep in mind I had been meeting hundreds and thousands of people on my travels with Lime. I was getting feedback from people like me who had also stayed away from disability. They would say things like, "Rich, you've changed my life, you've impacted me so much, keep doing what you're doing"—the kind of stuff that gets my wife all teary-eyed. Jenn has a name for it: she calls it a "standout moment."

So yes, all those standout moments constitute another thing, another driver, although I wouldn't call it the primary driver. You've learned by now that part of my positioning is to avoid the emotional, social side of disability in our business, while appreciating the personal connections and mentoring that are part of my life. That's why it's not laced throughout this book you're reading. Many people make this about emotion and saving the world. While commendable, that approach produces poor results. To differentiate, I've gone 180 degrees away from that to be as cold, calculating, and data-driven as I can be. We can use the levers and tools of economics—if applied correctly—to create the social value everyone desires as a direct result of broad economic success.

CHAPTER TWENTY-TWO
GETTING REAL ABOUT THE ECONOMICS OF DISABILITY

I n this chapter, I want to share the story of how I discovered the hidden economic juggernaut embodied by people with disabilities. I will let you in on how attracting PWD as a source of talent and smart consumers is a win-win-win for companies, investors, and more than a billion PWD. Exactly how did we build an investment fund that beats the Standard & Poor's 500, Wall Street's most famous index? I'll talk about our work with PepsiCo and other global brands in designing innovative approaches to marketing and merchandising to PWD and core consumers. You know what, *these* are the ideas I want you to remember from this book—not how I walk or what goofy people say to me in the airport.

I am working to help people and institutions understand that if we make unlocking the value in PWD a mandate about compliance or charity, business and government will not act on what's different and valuable. If you serve demand with the right supply, markets will clear. They always do—eventually. Because of that positioning, I have put a few noses out of joint. I'm aware of that. I take that as an indication that I'm doing something right. If I'm not pissing a few people off, I'm probably not doing it right. My challenge to those opposed to this approach? Do it better. I dare you. I also welcome you. Look, the water's fine over here on the market-driven side. Come on in. Let me be crystal clear—it will take a global army acting together to fix this broken model.

When I launched Return on Disability, I still didn't understand how I was going to apply the concepts and models that I had built. I knew that if my calculations were right, even if I got much of it wrong, it would *still* be successful. When you are first to market in a pool this size, if you have the background and the will to succeed, you will figure out the details. I could have been wrong. I still could be. *What if this wasn't as big as you thought it was?* I ask myself. It's possible. I mean, I was the only one coming up with these numbers. When I first started crunching these numbers in 2005, I could not cite U.S. Census data or existing benchmarks other than a fuzzy UN number of six hundred million PWD that didn't include China and India.

I force myself to acknowledge that I could be wrong, that I could have misjudged the market size. In spectacular fashion. My initial population number was 1.1 billion PWD globally versus the UN figure of six hundred million. How did I get my number? Basic math. The U.S. Census says that 18.7 percent of the population above five years old self-identifies as having a disability. Hey, what's five hundred million people between friends? The UN complex now quotes "over a billion" PWD. As an analyst, you want to be careful of being too optimistic. The first thing they teach you in Accounting 101 is the concept of conservatism. You don't want to be Pollyannaish; you don't want to overesti-mate the numbers and look foolish. There's a fine line between optimism and fraud. How do you tell the difference between a fraudster and an optimist? The cheat's usually in jail. The fact that I was putting out numbers that nobody had put out before carried significant risk in and of itself. I don't think that anyone had even considered trying that. No debate—if you trust the U.S. Census, then this is the number.

Developing the macro side, framing the market, was one of my first jobs. The 1.3 billion we quote now, which in 2005 was 1.1 billion, includes China and India. The UN had excluded China and India from their data because at that time their governments didn't officially recognize PWD and had no data on them as a distinct group—a minor oversight, right? It shows how far we've moved since I started this. Now China is getting serious about this, India is getting serious about this; these countries are beginning to move into the spaces that the West has been in for thirty years. Understand that's within my lifetime.

In an analysis of the Canadian disability market that was published in Canada's *Globe and Mail* in September 2017, I outlined that 18.7 percent of the Canadian population that self-declare as PWDs make an average annual income of 91 percent compared with those living without a disability. They make 91 cents on the dollar to a temporarily able-bodied worker.

Simple math says that six-plus million Canadians with a disability control $55.4 billion in annual disposable income. When we add friends and family to the equation, disability touches about half of all consumers, controlling more than $366.5 billion. That's just in Canada, folks.

I will admit that I could have timed the launch of Return on Disability better. It was the hardest thing I have ever done or ever will do. Full stop. And March 2008 was a challenging environment in which to start a new business. I was knocking on doors of companies that were worth half of what they were a few months before, asking for $100,000 to do an emerging market engagement that they had never heard of, in a way that they had never considered. It's not a formula for success. I had to knock on more than one or two doors.

Of course, nobody knew what was coming. Strangely, the most significant financial meltdown since the Great Depression turned out to be the perfect, *perfect* time for me to make my move. Think about it: if I had held on, I wouldn't have gotten paid at Merrill because nobody got paid; the company ended up imploding, and I got out ahead of it. I would love to say that was intentional, that I knew everything that was coming—I didn't—but I did see that it was highly unlikely that I was going to make a lot of money in the next few years. I was very bearish. And my thinking was *If there was ever a time to jump, it's now.* It was a gut feeling.

I had not anticipated the ramifications of what was coming: how was I going to call on Fortune 500 companies when the recession had cut their value in half? Some of my best prospects, the banks, were worth less than 10 percent of what they had been six months beforehand. *Ten percent.* Those were tough calls; nobody wanted to have anything to do with me. Think about it: emerging markets define what risk is. Emerging markets are the new and different when everybody is going back to basics. When everybody is de-risking, and you're coming in saying, "Invest in an emerging market," you're going to hear a lot of crickets and see a lot of tumbleweeds. I saw my fair share of crickets and tumbleweeds. It was a very lonely place for a long time.

I did have the time to build. I wasn't sitting on my hands, waiting for the phone to ring. I was building research assets. I was building new models. I was building observations. I was building a robust database of what companies were doing. I was going out and peeking under the covers, so to speak, and seeing what was going on. Nobody was watching me. I could set any process the way that I wanted to set it. Had it been a good market, I would have gone a lot faster and the quality might have suffered because I would have had to compete. As it happened, nobody else was doing this. I was the only one taking the risk.

By the way, for any of you thinking about starting a business, take an honest self-assessment. If you can't sit alone with your thoughts, your fears, your economic needs, while keeping the mental picture of your vision for your business alive, reconsider taking the plunge. Because those moments will find you. What did F. Scott Fitzgerald write? That there are times when "in a real dark night of the soul it is always three o'clock in the morning, day after day." You'll have too many of those as an entrepreneur, and you need the fortitude to get through them.

The office part was where I made some mistakes as an entrepreneur. I thought I needed an office, so I went and rented one at Park Avenue and Fifty Seventh, in the same building where Richard Nixon had had his office before becoming president. It cost me $4,000 a month. What that got me was a tiny office with no window. Welcome to New York City. I had some money saved, so I could afford to do it. I left Merrill with a nice package, but that package goes away quickly, especially in New York, and even more especially when you're investing in a new business. When you have your own business, you never have enough cash. Ever. Clients pay slowly; vendors want money fast. Fast out, slow in means you have less cash than you think you have. Cash flow is oxygen for a business—especially a new one.

Coming from a culture of going to an office, I wasn't comfortable with sitting at home. I eventually ended up doing that anyhow because I got more work done and didn't have to spend $4,000 per month. Those are the mistakes you make opening your own business. I bought a new computer; I didn't need a new computer. I bought a new cell phone. I had to have everything new, new, new. Wrong, wrong, wrong. What I was selling was in my head. I burned through a lot of cash in those first two years.

This was before Jenn joined the business. Jenn's salary at Avon and our savings played a significant role in providing stability in those early years. For that, I am grateful. What I was embarking on was going to be big—but it might not have been, without Jenn's unwavering investment in me.

CHAPTER TWENTY-THREE
PEPSI, PLEASE

Three days after my last day at Merrill, The Return on Disability Group got its first customer: a small company called PepsiCo. They came on board March 18, 2008, the second day we opened our doors. And they have been with us ever since.

Our business relationship began with a call I had made the previous December. At that time, I was speaking with three people at Pepsi: Lynda Costa, Mike Mihok, and David Nail. So, I went out to meet with these three people and said, "Okay, let me ask you a question. You're entering this phase where you're starting to tackle disability, both on the recruiting side and on the customer side. Would you be interested in a service that marshaled you through that process?"

I started to sketch out what I was thinking, what I was doing, and they said, "Yeah, we would. Let us take it to our boss." So, they took it to the boss, and he said, "Yup, done."

By becoming our first client, and being patient with the development of new models and metrics, PepsiCo invested in a new concept that became the Return on Disability model. Together, we bootstrapped Return on Disability. I think they knew that the business world would need this work. We had an excellent relationship already; they knew what I could produce. I believe that half the reason they became a client was a desire to take a close look at this market; the other half was that they wanted to support me. Because of the support they showed me in the early days, you will never find a Coca-Cola product in my house. Mine is a Pepsi home; it will always be a Pepsi home. If this becomes what I think it will become, Pepsi deserves a lot of credit for being there early. You can't get there much earlier than that. Pepsi is not merely a customer; they are family.

I expect this relationship to remain strong. Pepsi's CEO, Indra Nooyi, has made it clear to the world and Pepsi's global team that it is not enough to compete on product and price. In part due to the rise of the millennial generation, who want brands to meet their changing demands around social actions, Pepsi is a leader among companies that "weave purpose into the core business of the company," as Nooyi has said. She believes that part of a chief executive's duty is to ensure that a company's business goals align with initiatives that meet or exceed these new consumer demands. Return on Disability takes performance with purpose to the next level. It simply factors "social action" into traditional demand-and-supply frameworks and provides an action set to maximize returns. It is not corporate social responsibility (CSR). It is not "being a good corporate citizen." It is a brand acting on the demands of a large and material customer base—people connected to disability.

As I settled into the new role, I was spending a lot of time at PepsiCo headquarters in Purchase, New York, knocking this about, figuring out how to attack it. Just before our engagement began, Pepsi produced a disability-related ad for the Super Bowl that was a huge hit. "Bob's House" won awards and got millions and millions of views on YouTube (check it out, just Google "Bob's House Super Bowl ad"). Pepsi was just starting to wake up to the potential of disability and what it could do for the bottom line. Marketers are always looking to create a strong emotional connection to their brand, and, in that context, disability is a marketer's dream. Whether you or someone in your family has a disability, the chances are high that you have a strong emotional response to the issues surrounding it. It goes to the core of who you are—complexity aside. Incredibly, many companies have yet to discover how they can better engage the disability market.

The ad was green-lighted by a gentleman named Massimo d'Amore, then CEO of PepsiCo's Global Beverages Group. I fell in love with the guy at the time, just an amazing genius at what he does. He had his share of controversy over rebranding that resulted in his leaving Pepsi in 2012. A risk taker. The man I knew was brilliant. He was the champion of disability at Pepsi, and six weeks into my engagement he wanted to test me. Massimo called up and said, "Come see me in Manhattan; I'll be at this address. Let's meet."

I had never met this guy in the flesh before, and I had no idea where we were meeting. I'm a finance guy, right? So here I am going to this office in the Village, in this big old converted warehouse. The elevator door opens, and there's this life-sized and strikingly authentic statue of Darth Vader standing in front of me. I'm thinking, *What have I gotten myself into?* I walk in and tell the receptionist who I am and that I'm here to see Massimo d'Amore and Peter Arnell. I'm thinking Peter is probably some vice-president. No, he's the owner of the ad agency that Massimo has chosen to host our meeting. By the way, there's no name on the door. No sign says "This is the Arnell Group." Massimo gave me an address and a floor number. I didn't even know that this *was* the Arnell Group.

So, I walk into reception and sit down right beside Darth Vader, who stands seven-foot-six. Looking back on it now, I find the irony hilarious. I get called into the conference room, and Massimo and Peter are waiting for me. I've never met either of them. Here I am, meeting with the CEO of Global Beverages for Pepsi, probably the number three guy at the company, Arnell's biggest client, and the head of this prestigious Manhattan ad agency.

Arnell's trying to impress his client, I'm trying to impress my potential client, and I imagine they're both trying to figure out who the hell I am. I know my job is to explain to Massimo what the disability market is. Up until now he's been thinking of this as a CSR issue. He was thinking with the heart. My job is to get him thinking with his head. I take him through my presentation, and Arnell's firing all these questions at me—great questions—and I'm coming right back at him with "No, you're thinking about it wrong. It's this way; it's that way." I have no idea that I'm talking to one of the most demanding bosses in the ad industry—hence the Darth Vader statue. I'm coming back at him strong because I don't know all that; to me, he's a smart guy I want to win over.

We are having this intense conversation that goes on for about an hour when Arnell says, "All right, you've got me sold. I'm buying; this is real." Of course, I go back later, I do my research and find out that Peter Arnell sits on the board of Special Olympics. He has been trying to convince Massimo to get Pepsi into Special Olympics as a sponsor, and I've been advising against it. I was saying things like, "You don't want to be riding on that brand because it's yesterday's way of doing things." So, this, I now understood, was my test. If you can hang with Arnell, you can hang with anybody.

Arnell's career was a rollercoaster in the years after that meeting; he was let go from Omnicom, and his reputation as a boss is less than flattering. With me, he was engaging, smart, and fair.

After the meeting, Massimo offered me a lift since he was

going uptown. As we got into his car, he said, "By the way, you were fantastic in that meeting. I've never seen anybody push back on him the way you did. It was fabulous." He said, "Let me ask you one question. If we hire you at PepsiCo as an adviser, what do you want to accomplish by the end of your tenure?"

"That's very simple, Massimo," I said. "In three to five years I want you to be able to say, 'PepsiCo beat its numbers this quarter because of its activity in the disability market.' And you would repeat that line every quarter for five years. That's why we're doing this." Massimo drove me to the office and said, "Okay, do a proposal, tell me how you want to get paid, I'm not picky, just make it very clear, and we'll get this done." And for me that was game on. Until then I had an agreement in principle; now I had an official sign-on.

After that it became real. For a new business, that was a speedy turnaround, because these deals can take months to close. This one took about six weeks. It was a payday, but more than that I was beginning to understand what I had. If I could convince Darth Vader as well as probably one of the biggest minds in branding, d'Amore, that I had something real, and they were buying it—because they didn't need to buy it; it wasn't a charity conversation—then it was real. It became real for me that day. Jenn and I enjoyed a bottle of champagne on the roof deck that night to celebrate. That was a fun day. A day I would live again over the coming ten years.

The process of isolating what Return on Disability would deliver started at Pepsi. The challenge was acting within a specific brand. At a corporation that had twenty-two brands with at least $1 billion in annual revenue and operations in almost every country in the world, employing three hundred thousand people, with products on shelves in every store you could think of, that represents a significant operational challenge. We had to find the right people and have the right conversations. I would later understand this to be the most important part of our core sales process. We started quickly on packaging and did a couple of messaging projects. That resulted in Pepsi designing all its packaging for cans around disability. When you look at a pack of Pepsi cans today, I had a hand in designing them.

We began by creating guardrails for innovation around disability. I prefer thinking of our functional models as guardrails, not rules, as they allow the space for creativity while acting as protective barriers for the brand's core attributes. They empower designers to enhance their creative process while allowing significant design freedom. Still, I wanted to seed the brains of designers to think in a certain way, in a particular direction, but without prescribing and curbing creativity. That is critical, because if you are prescriptive, you will get bad design. When you're dealing with a PepsiCo or an Apple, whose product is dependent on great design, you can't mess around.

"Wait a sec," you may ask, "how is selling soda dependent on design?"

My answer? It's totally dependent on superior design and marketing. Pepsi is water, bubbles, and flavor, just like Coca-Cola is water, bubbles, and flavor. Delighting customers is the path to revenue growth. A core part of the customer experience is the refreshing product itself, but the bubbly liquid is only a part of that experience. End to end, a consumer follows many steps between considering the need for refreshment and "disposing" of the residual implements after enjoying a cold Pepsi-Cola. The steps in between can be analyzed and adjusted to improve that experience and ultimately grow revenue. The Return on Disability Group asks PWD how to make these steps easier to take and helps companies leverage these learnings to build better experiences for both PWD and core consumers. It does not take a rocket scientist to deduce that "easier to use" improves core consumer experience. This is the core revenue driver of Return on Disability for firms that face a broad consumer base.

In the retail product environment, design and packaging are critical to customer delight. In our case, we knew customer experience was core to Pepsi's business and we would fail as advisers if we were overly prescriptive. My team can't possibly understand their brand as they do. That's why we call them guardrails. You can go over a guardrail easily, but you must intentionally decide to do it. If there's a good reason to do it, that's a valid decision.

What I find—and this is fascinating to me—is that the simple existence of these guardrails causes designers to use them to drive their design. It's new; it's fun; it doesn't feel onerous; it feels more like a suggestion than a rule. As a designer focused on customer experience, you're going to say, *Hey, I can use this to make my designs better for everyone.* When design drives creation, magic happens. I've seen it. We have done it with Pepsi, over and over.

Delivering these guardrails involved a presentation to senior management at PepsiCo who run the beverages business. We were in the main boardroom on the fourth floor of Building Six in the PepsiCo complex in Purchase. So we got into this boardroom with six people, including Massimo d'Amore and Simon Lowden, the chief marketing officer of Beverages North America at the time. I gave them my stump presentation, the one I always give to educate new people—Simon was seeing this for the first time. But I wanted to do something theatrical.

We were talking about packaging. I said, "Look, packaging is probably the easiest way for you guys to activate. It's concrete, you're going to reinvent your packages every so often, so let's leverage the disability-use case to innovate." They were interested, but I didn't have them yet. "Do you want to know what it takes for me to open a can of Pepsi?" I asked. I reached into my man-purse, pulled out a straw, put it on the table, pulled out a standard table knife from my kitchen, put it on the table. I grabbed a can of Pepsi from the middle of the table—because, obviously, we're at Pepsi, so guess what they're going to put on the table to drink—and put the can in front of me. I stood up and pushed my chair all the way back to the wall. I took a few steps back so that I wasn't hidden from view by the table. I got down on my knees, grabbed the can of Pepsi, stuck it between my knees, grabbed the knife, leveraged it under the tab, pulled up on it, the can opens, I get a little bit wet, and at that point I said, "I usually don't get wet, but I thought it would be more impactful." Everybody was probably uncomfortable by this point, right? I got the straw, stuck it in my teeth, bent over, stuck the other end in the can and sucked half of it back. As I straightened up, I said, "Guys, if you can make it easier for me to open a can of Pepsi, you can make it easier for everybody to open a can of Pepsi."

I have told that story many ways around the world. It is pure theater, but it is also real. I still open a can of Pepsi the same way today. There is a good reason why cans are made the way they are, driven by cost, but there will come a point when that changes. Disability will drive that change. When packaging technology gets to the point where it's no longer too costly to change the basic design of the can, that will happen.

I've got dozens of ideas on how we can make it easier to open cans, but I'm not about to prescribe them. Pepsi is aware of this challenge and is continuing to white-board options for making it easier for people with dexterity issues to open their packages. Remember what I said. Change doesn't swoop out of the sky like a magic flying eagle. It takes hard, consistent work, communication, good design and effective production techniques, all of it. Three yards and a cloud of dust. Physical access is an issue for a small percentage of people in the marketplace. Addressing cognitive issues has a much greater impact on both PWD and the core consumer.

Return on Disability has quietly helped Pepsi out with the Super Bowl since 2012. Pepsi has a partnership with the National Association of the Deaf (NAD) to translate the national anthem into American Sign Language for the game. For a few years, they didn't know what to do with it. They had kids doing it, they had choirs—all noble efforts but off brand for Pepsi. So a few years ago, I said, "What if we went weird? What if we found a character who would better represent the Pepsi brand of fun/sexy/cool?" NAD found the actor John Maucere, who is the spitting image of Ron Burgundy from *Anchorman*. He's just a character. So he comes on and does this incredible rendition of the national anthem. It gets picked up by TMZ.com. Pepsi received sixty million hits on top of the Super Bowl hits, which ultimately resulted in $4 million worth of earned advertising. Simply by staying on brand in the disability market.

In the case of beverage packaging and related products, people with disabilities are "lead users." I was honored to work with Columbia Business School, Professor Olivier Toubia, then student Nithya Raman (now at Google Singapore), and PepsiCo on a formal lead user case study about retail innovation. A lot of what Pepsi does with its retail customers is to create solutions. They will come up with concepts for Walmart or Loblaws or Walgreens that will drive traffic and grow revenue. Nithya and I researched what Pepsi could do to attract consumers with disabilities in the retail innovation arena. We identified people with disabilities as lead users—a term coined by MIT management professor Eric von Hippel to describe consumers who recognize a need before it exists in the market.

While PWDs represent 18.7 percent of the consumer market for Pepsi, their needs are emerging in a way that will be important to a much larger population. Pepsi, in this case, has an inside track on product solutions that will become a competitive edge as the market grows. I have issues getting my fingers to do what I want them to—causing me to avoid a career as a brain surgeon. So will tens of millions of baby boomers aging in the years ahead. Lead users—in this case, PWD—offer a source of ideas and innovation.

Columbia Business School now teaches this case in its curriculum. That put both Pepsi and Columbia Business School right at the edge of innovation in disability and made me one proud alum. I hope to see other graduate schools and students bring academic rigor to the business issues driven by the disability market. It's far more involved than charity races and fundraisers; it must be, if we want to unlock the value in people with disabilities.

Those are the kinds of things that we do with Pepsi. For other clients, we spent a lot of time educating them and socializing the idea of Return on Disability. Our job begins with getting leaders to buy in and start acting in ways that create shareholder value. The Return on Disability model you will read about now drives everything, but it was still taking shape during our initial journey with PepsiCo in 2008 and 2009.

By late 2009, things were moving. We were doing some work on packaging, some work on advertising in the various brands, we had three ads in the hopper, we had agencies going on different concepts. These are process-driven creative services, meaning that there would be an asset left behind if I got hit by a bus. Clients know the typical consultant mistake: when you walk in, you are the show. Today the client wants to know that if you were to walk away, there would still be some corporate assets left behind, that they can execute without you. That kind of thinking makes a lot of people in my position nervous, but for me it's an imperative. Remember, I'm not here just to make a buck, although it's nice if we deliver results. I'm here to incite corporate behavioral change. Because if I do that, I will unlock value, and I will see part of that. Pay comes after production. In that I trust. If I provide value, I will eventually get paid for it.

About that time, my job at Pepsi changed. I started quantifying how the Return on Disability initiative would look in three years' time, in five years' time, and how Pepsi could step from one level to the next. I was working closely with Lynda Costa, a quality guru and process improvement expert. Lynda speaks the language of Six Sigma. She understands total quality management. She understands benchmarking; she understands gap analysis—everything that Return on Disability was becoming. We started out by converting the 302 touchpoints I had written down over a year earlier into a model for use in driving corporate process on disability. We evaluated each touchpoint on whether it increased revenue and/or decreased cost—the two drivers of shareholder value. In the private sector, you make change faster when your actions are growing revenues or cutting costs.

We boiled the 302 touchpoints to thirty factors and weighted them differently depending on their impact on value creation. We measure things like customer experience and messaging to both customers and employees. Simple. The Return on Disability model was born. We now use it in every analysis that we do. Every company that we analyze gets a score based on how they perform on those thirty data points, which we divide into three umbrella categories. Those categories are: a) customer: how a company attracts the disability market to their products and services to grow revenue; b) talent: how a company recruits, hires, and promotes employees with disabilities to cut costs; and c) productivity: how a company leverages disability to drive efficient processes that ultimately cut costs.

Getting the data we need involves a significant amount of research. We go to stores and online, look at marketing materials, buy the products, and experience the services. We visit the head offices; we walk/roll right into the lobby, ask to see a random person, analyze what that experience is like as both a customer and a prospective employee. To date, I have visited more Walmarts and bank branches than any human being should. Evaluating the employment and recruiting sector is easier for us to do. We apply for jobs. We visit their job site, fill in applications, call them up, determine how the company is attracting people. The internet is a great facilitator of efficient talent research. Between Google and YouTube, we can see five years' worth of advertising in twenty minutes reasonably easily. I don't know if the RoD process would even be possible without the internet. Aside from head office and retail site visits, getting the observations is not difficult, just time-consuming. Once we figured out a baseline process over the first three years, we could repeat it at scale.

We use a binary process for evaluating and including or not including a company in the Return on Disability Stock Market Index. That is, I don't want to get into a value debate over whether one activity is better than another. If there is activity in a category, you get a 1. If you don't, you get a 0. That's binary. We can get away with the simplicity of that approach because it reflects reality and because there are so few players acting in ways that create value. As the activity ramps up over the next five years, we will change the methodology. That will not be difficult: since 2010, we have been privately running a more complex parallel methodology that our customers have been enjoying. But because this is so new, simple is better than complex in public. The binary method is easy to explain and consistent across every data set. So the only thing that's discretionary are the observations. I have years of experience observing disability activity, but also years of building an understanding of what to look for, what to measure, and how to measure it.

I wouldn't call the Return on Disability external analysis process an academic exemplar, diving into minute detail, but that is deliberate. A customer in the real world is not going to spend a lot of time testing these things out, nor do they care about minutiae. If you're going to have an impact on your customer, any action taken must be easily noticeable, even obvious. Customers are not going to dig through the back of the store to find out how you can help them. It must be part of the experience; it must be quick and easy. That's what we are looking for when we test what a company is doing. The difference between a sale and no sale from a consumer in the disability market can be a simple shift of activity—and it often is.

I had a chief diversity officer for a significant payments company call me three or four years ago. She said, "Hey, Rich, just a question for you. I spent $3 million over two years developing these wonderful disability policies. I've got twenty-six volumes of policy on my desk. Why are we not in the index?"

"Simple question," I said. "Can your customers see that? Do those policies impact the customer?"

"Well, no."

"Then why did you do it?" I asked. "I would argue that twenty-six volumes of policies are creating a cost for you because you have to dust them off every year. They're not impacting your business. Congratulations on the policies, but they give you no credit on my analysis, because they don't impact your customers or your employees."

She meant well, but she had wasted $3 million of shareholder value. Worse, I think that the focus on policy creates a mindset of *Hey, we can wash our hands now. We've got the policies, look in the policy book. If we ever get sued or audited, we're okay.* I think that is complete and utter bullshit, and shareholders should demand business results from all efforts. The funny thing is that this payment company had technology that scored high on improving experience driven by disability. Their tap payment cards are easy to use; they're fantastic. But this company was not talking about that. In a nod to competitive forces, another payment gateway company scores well on the Return on Disability model because they talk about tap cards as an ease-of-use driver. They have precisely the same technology. One talks about it; one doesn't—thus creating two very different customer experiences. Hint: the company that talks about disability as an ease-of-use driver scores higher on the Return on Disability model.

By educating these companies and guiding them to act on robust business strategies, we're helping them to understand the folly of the charity and regulatory mindset around disability. The community mentality that charities have sold corporations (and governments) is doing a great deal of damage not only to shareholder value but also to the disability market and PWD themselves. In environmental terms, the charities are green-washing disability. All talk, no material action. I don't think that is intentional. I don't think they are out to cause harm; they just don't have any concept of identity from an economic or social context. People don't think the right way in large part because a lot of diversity isn't market-based but rather is compliance-based. It has its roots in affirmative action, in which you need to set hiring quotas for specific groups. Great companies are beginning to understand that mistake. They are looking at the market opportunities not only in disability but also in other diversity markets. We have started to call these "non-traditional markets."

When it comes to disability, compliance is the reason why America is doing better than Canada. The scores I am seeing are remarkably better in America, which has been playing the market game, than in Canada, which has been playing the compliance game for three decades. In the U.S., the quantity of activity is lower, but the quality is higher. I think that is going to flip-flop in the next five years. The quality in Canada is going to rise because most companies are starting to move on from compliance to focus on market-driven activity. The best Canadian firms have realized that a compliance focus has failed, costing the Big Five Canadian banks more than $250 million since 1989. Failure looks like sixty PWD hires a year on an employee base of eighty thousand and no focus on customer experience. Three of the five banks in Canada have started to engage in a market-based approach in the last five years, with varying levels of early results.

The U.S. Department of Labor added new guidelines in 2013 to the law protecting PWD from discrimination on the part of U.S. federal contractors and subcontractors. This law is known as Section 503, and the additional guidelines required more reporting, disclosure, paperwork, and compliance. Section 503 also suggested a hiring quota—or "target"—for PWD of 7 percent of a company's workforce. (Currently, large companies have an average of 1 to 2 percent of their workforce as disclosed PWD.) These regulations blunt market-driven initiatives among employers who believe *We must comply with this* and will do the minimum to keep the feds out of their hair. I don't know about you, but I am not that excited about joining a company that only wants me as a quota number. It is just not attractive to me as a prospect. If you *do* attract people with disabilities, they will disclose, and your numbers will improve. It is a catch-22 for companies. Compliance in Canada was supposed to help PWD, and it resulted in literally billions of dollars spent with little results. Quotas do not work, because they incent the wrong behavior from employers.

Fortunately, our work and those of the few other savvy players in the field, such as Lime Connect, have kept the momentum alive. New compliance burdens at best muddy the waters on how to act on PWD to compete and thrive in a global economy. At worst, 503 incents "cover your butt" behavior that will drive talented people with disabilities to go work for a company that values them as agents of success. Counterproductive regulations draw away precious leadership attention and reinforce ridiculous stereotypes that PWD can't contend without regulatory crutches —and so, therefore, are in some ways less qualified. Perception is reality until proven otherwise.

Data over time tracks progress, which is why I'm big on measurement. You can measure anything and determine whether changes observed are a good thing or a bad thing. For me, the magic of Return on Disability is the weighting, which we index to shareholder value. It is indexed to neither disability nor activity level. It looks at financial performance in the same way business people do.

Look at Walgreens, for example. The company is well known for its hiring program. It is also an A-list example of how to execute the productivity metric. Walgreens leverages the disability experience to drive productive assets. The company began employing PWD in its distribution centers as a "nice to do" effort. To their surprise, Walgreens discovered that when you put PWD into an assembly-type situation, they simplify things. They must. People with disabilities, whether physical or cognitive, must find workarounds: type is replaced with colors, numbers with symbols. Where people had been walking a hundred feet, they reduced the distance to two.

In adapting the job to the individual, Walgreens stumbled across one of the most potent lean process tools around. Employing PWD in their distribution centers cut annual operating costs by 20 percent. Put another way, after thirty years of standard hiring practices, Walgreens discovered that taking on PWD exposed so-called able-bodied people as remarkably slow and inefficient.

A big win. Walgreens took the complexity out; they drove down costs, they got better results. Good as it is, though, it doesn't drive much value. People always ask me, "How did Walgreens score?" They think it's going to be one of the best companies in the research universe. Walgreens continues to make the top one hundred scoring companies in the U.S. on the RoD metric, but it lags behind companies like Disney and Pepsi, who are focused on serving their customers. Delighting the customer is where the value is for these companies. Employees don't drive revenue in a retail environment. They help. They're part of that conversation, but hiring practices don't drive shareholder value for consumer-facing firms. Marketing, branding, product development, and customer experience are the factors that drive value for a retailer.

Investing in a skilled, engaged, and efficient workforce is part of running a good business. But the reality is, it's not the biggest part. In a company like Walgreens, you don't spend much time at an investor conference talking about HR policy. Investors care about where your sales are, what you're doing to grow, what you're doing to push revenue up, what you're doing to push revenue up, and oh, by the way, what are you doing to push revenue up?

Walgreens' productivity enhancements driven by PWD add $44 million annually to the bottom line. That's not an insignificant sum, but Walgreens had $117.4 billion in revenue for 2016; $44 million is nice, but it's not going to make much of an impact on their business. If Walgreens was paying close attention, it would concentrate on better serving its customers with disabilities. If they shift 0.02 percent of their revenue away from their competition by delighting disability-linked consumers, they will outpace their current $44 million cost savings. Delighting customers is the real value creation opportunity for Walgreens and for the majority of large companies today. Actions that may be taken by Walgreens can range from on-brand portrayals of customers with disabilities in advertising to serious efforts to make shopping easier for everyone.

CHAPTER TWENTY-FOUR
ENGINEERING A NEW STOCK INDEX

In late 2009 I got the idea of applying the thirty-touchpoint Return on Disability analysis to all the companies in the S&P 500. (As defined by Investopedia, the Standard & Poor's 500 "is an index of 500 stocks issued by 500 large companies with market capitalizations of at least $6.1 billion. It is seen as a leading indicator of U.S. equities and a reflection of the performance of the large-cap universe." Numerous investment products are based on the S&P because these blue-chip companies shape and reflect the direction of the U.S. economy.) I figuratively locked myself in a room for six months and went through the entire S&P, analyzing how the biggest five hundred companies listed on U.S. exchanges acted on disability.

The first research cycle was lighter than the process is now; I performed far fewer site visits than we do today. I wanted to get a baseline on the level of activity in the marketplace. I hypothesized that if you put together a portfolio of one hundred companies that did disability well, they would beat the market. I figured that if they did disability well, they were responsive companies that delivered on customer and employee demands better than their competition.

By about the third month of researching the S&P 500, my brain was fried. I was repeating the Return on Disability process for five hundred companies. I wanted to do it all myself because there is no better way to become an expert than to create data from scratch. Since Pepsi was my only client at that point, I had the time to do it.

Six to eight months later, I had developed a list of 140 out of 500 companies that had demonstrated measurable progress in business practices and activities that affect people with disabilities. I found that about forty of these companies were higher performers, which meant and still means scoring at least two points on a scale of five. Not spectacular results, but from a data point of view I had built something robust. Only two or three firms that I analyzed at that time could be described as excellent in disability, but I found clear differentiation among the stronger players. Disney was stronger, Pepsi was stronger, a couple of the banks were doing some interesting things. But it wasn't an overwhelming number of companies.

It was also clear that no company was performing in a way that indicated that they understood the opportunity. This finding excited me because it meant that the bulk of the opportunity was still available to businesses. It also told me that various groups giving out awards for "excellence" or "perfect" scores on copycat "indices" were bogus. Self-surveys and "pay-to-play" lists and "certifications" are vehicles that charities and lobbyists were (and still are) using to raise money and create the illusion of activity. Data has a funny way of exposing bullshit. True, my data could be wrong—but someone would need to improve my approach to argue that. That's why ruthlessly independent rigor based on measurable data from repeatable models draws so much attention in the "social" sphere. It creates a rational space for dialogue where rhetoric doesn't cut it, and better data is the price of entry. Evidence-based practices have reshaped medicine and management because they give professionals a common platform of verified facts and findings.

In my field, we need less emotional assertion and more evidence-based discussion. Some attention-grabbers can get clicks on the internet by saying childhood vaccines are a conspiracy or that America faked the moon landing. Others insist the Earth is flat and are building a rocket to prove it (true story, friend). But no one's inviting them to a serious discussion. Almost all of us acknowledge that facts aren't relative or in the eye of the beholder. Truth is truth, math is math. So if other experts want to compete with our methodology, as I said, come on in, the water's fine. But to do so successfully, they will need to build a better model than ours, not just make stuff up. Competing on quality means better outcomes for PWD in the end—a good thing. And this is the whole point.

So, the initial index analysis. I took the one hundred top rated companies, cut them into an equal-weighted basket, and compared them with the S&P 500. I found they performed significantly better than the S&P: 2 to 3 percent better year over year, with the same level of risk. In my world, that's worth paying attention to. Three percent, with the same risk as the index? As an investor, I would do that trade every day. Most investors wouldn't think twice about that.

Staring at that spreadsheet, I knew I had something valuable. Once again, I didn't realize how big of a deal that result was, but I knew it was real. And I knew I had a platform that I could take to any company in the marketplace. Jenn was very patient waiting for me to emerge from the long dark tunnel of this time, and I could not have kept my hairline intact without her.

I brought Dustin on as a partner to help me shape disability as a marketplace. A lot of the thinking behind the consumer identity embedded in the Return on Disability of today is thanks to Dustin's ability to position disability from a brand perspective. I'm a finance guy, not a brand guru. He helped me understand why identity was so critical to binding all of disability into one market. The problem with this marketplace is that policymakers and charities always have fragmented people by condition: CP, MS, DS, ADHD, dyslexia, on and on and on. That's the only way that the disability market has ever been cut: by specific disability—by medical diagnosis. It was becoming clear to me that a condition-based approach was never going to be successful. Practically, as a company, you can't possibly serve sixty-five or more different conditions. It's just not going to work.

More importantly, the diagnosis does not equal PWD identity from a consumer or employee point of view. Identity has more to do with how people interact with brands, experiences, and one's expected outcomes relative to functional differences caused by disability—whether the differences are real or perceived. Experience in a store in no way depends on medical diagnosis.

That's the general principle behind Return on Disability. We don't look at medical condition; we look at functionality: how people interact with products, services, and the companies that produce them. PWD want the same—or better—experiences and products everybody else does. They want to spend their money on what creates delight. The ability to find the common factors across all these disabilities is critical.

This approach from consumer identity reframed how we talk about disability. That is just as important in business as it is in politics. Rather than "Hey, how many people with autism did you hire this year?" or "What charity do you write checks to?" Identity got us talking about PWD as a market—a common body, a force in the economy, and a vibrant army for your talent base.

Bonding a market by functionality and identity as opposed to dividing it by condition? It makes sense intuitively, but it needed a framework. For marketers, that's their language, and you need to be able to speak it to get them on board. When I present to a brand manager, they come into the meeting thinking, *How am I going to attack this market by condition?* and they walk out thinking, *Oh. I get it. That's easy.* Of course, there is more to it than that. However, that initial framing is a critical first step.

By replacing the taxonomy of condition with that of identity and functionality, we do something essential for disability. We elevate it from individual circumstances to the same level as any other market. We are no longer talking about a sliver of the disability marketplace; we are talking about all of it.

From a corporate point of view, the perceived difference between gender/race and disability is that, with some exceptions, disability often requires a functional adaptation to deliver an experience that is equal to or better than the "norm." This is true, although in 90 percent of cases that adaptation is simple. For the other groups, the adaptations are largely about perception, not requiring a change in design. The most constructive way to look at this is that if you can make a functional change for people with disabilities, you can improve things for everybody at the same time. We have come to learn over the years that the same philosophy we follow for PWD can be applied to any segment— arguably the biggest "aha" moment in my professional life.

An excellent illustration of this mindset comes from Japan. Faced with an aging population that has trouble distinguishing the various kanji (text characters), Japanese policymakers and designers are moving from text on signs to icons (pictures). That makes for some funny bathroom signs, but it also makes for a wonderfully efficient communication technique. If you go to a grocery store in North America, the signs above the aisles are all in text. If you don't read English or you don't see very well, or you process information differently for some reason, those signs fail to meet your expectations as a customer. An icon, picture, or some other functional element that gives you an idea of what's down the aisle is far more effective and efficient than a white word on a black sign.

Exchanging condition for functionality also gives companies the ability to make everything consistent. They don't need to reinvent things when they refresh designs or apply a novel approach to the enterprise. They have a language; they have a scalable system that they can employ in every context in which they do business, across every line of business.

After I did our analysis of the S&P 500, I started to look at how we could bring it to market. I realized that if firms could earn a higher return by serving their customers and pass those profits on to investors, it would quickly change the face of disability. It's one thing for me to stand up and suggest that a CEO change her firm's behavior; it's an entirely different conversation if an investor demands it.

If I am a chief investment officer at a large pension fund holding one hundred million shares of stock in Microsoft, and I have invested in the Return on Disability Index, on my quarterly or semiannual call with the CEO of Microsoft, I'm going to say, "Satya, I just invested in the RoD stock index. What are you guys doing on disability?" Watch the fur fly. Suddenly it's not somebody pushing a string up a hill, it's the CEO of Microsoft calling his direct reports saying, "I just got a call from a major investor asking me what are we doing in disability. I want to see a report on my desk in a week. If we need to do better, please come to me with a plan." Being a good CEO, he will then hold his team accountable to that plan. This is how companies operate.

What I am trying to do is to instill a sense of competition into companies. I want them to aspire to be in the index for financial reasons as well as for market-driven bragging rights. It is not difficult to get into the index today—it requires basic knowledge and publicly demonstrating genuine effort. Over time that benchmark will get higher, and eventually every company will have such a burning desire to be in the Return on Disability Index that they will improve their performance in disability. Embedded in that spirit of competition are actions that serve customers with a disability and spur employers to hire and promote employees with disabilities—a social goal with which few people would argue. That's what this is: a market-driven incentive to change corporate behavior. Socially responsible investing has failed to get investors to pick up the phone and call companies and say, "Hey, we just put $100 million into XYZ Fund, what are you doing in this space?" Well, that's not entirely true. It happens in a tiny way. Return on Disability is meant to do this on a large scale, focusing on those things that cause companies to change their behavior. That is all it is intended to do. It's going to work. It's just a question of how long it takes to happen.

The "green" market is a good example of how competitive pressures create change. Tree huggers have been around for more than forty-five years. They circulate petitions; they try to board ships and climb bridges; they send out animal calendars and commission reports and make news. They do their best to get people's attention, and they believe in their cause. A few nationally elected officials developed serious expertise and listened to scientists. But for many years, the average Joe wasn't listening. It wasn't until the *Exxon Valdez* oil spill in 1989 that the mass market started to pay attention. Suddenly, if you were a consumer brand, there was a benefit to activating on green. People were willing to pay more for "green" products, sales went up, and green became a critical part of value. Guess what? Every company did it. Now we are starting to see the benefits.

This change-through-competition has come to pass in every other vertical, and it will be no different in disability. The twist is investors have never had a system of environmental, social, and governance (ESG) investing driven by direct links to actual returns to shareholders. Social good currently drives impact investing more than returns. It has always been based on things that don't really have anything to do with value. "Are you carbon-neutral?" "Do you have at least two independent directors on your board of directors?" "Do you produce guns?" "What is the percentage of women on your board of directors?" Investors struggle to relate these factors to higher returns—and rightly so.

Return on Disability shows companies what the disability market—one that forms about half of the population—can do to drive up the value of their shares. If a company scores well, they will outpace their competition, delivering higher revenue and lower cost. That is because we have linked the factors we measure directly to value creation, not tangentially to social value. Yes, social value is built by serving and hiring, but its creation is a result of acting in the interests of shareholders. We have converted a cause into a market.

That's new to social investing. In fact, our market-first philosophy is not that popular with some in the sector. I'm sure that there is a picture of me on the back of someone's door with a dart right between the eyes. Because I'm calling them out. I'm saying, "You need to deliver returns for shareholders first to move this forward." The social benefits come because of acting on an economic opportunity. By serving returns, they will also serve a social benefit because they will be improving the lives of PWD via increased economic participation. I believe that promoting social interest through value is the way that everything will be done in this space. Good old-fashioned market forces.

If we can have the CIO of CalPERS (California Public Employees' Retirement System) or the CIO of the University of Michigan investment fund calling the head of Google saying, "We're thrilled with what you're doing in disability, keep going, do more," that will change Google's behavior. If Warren Buffett calls the CEO of Coke and says, "Hey, Pepsi is kicking your ass in disability. Why are you lagging behind?" that would change Coke's behavior.

Until the consumer and investor believe something and act on it, the conversation is never going to lead to action. It's just not. Change occurs when you have consumer demand driving change heightened by investor demand. That's the proven combination.

That is how you shorten a twenty-year period of organic change into a five-year period of activist change. That is what we are doing with RoD: leveraging the Return on Disability Index to push company behavior from the investors down, while at the same time getting companies to listen to and meet consumer demand by improving the ways that they address disability.

We are doing this out of self-interest, yes. I own a business whose success is tied to getting this right. I am also a PWD, so better experiences benefit me too. But above all, we see a signifi-cant economic dislocation that must be corrected. We will not tap the level of talent required to change the face of disability unless we can show the financial rewards and prove to rational economic actors that behavior change is in their interest. Today, there are not enough talented people flocking to this space. To attract the brightest brains in the world, who can do anything they want with their time, you have to offer something that's lucrative. When you prove that value, you will attract thousands of quality people, and I will attract competitors, which is just fine. I can't do this by myself. It's too big.

The third piece, which is missing, is empowering consumers to pull companies in a direction. We have investors pushing and corporations supplying a demand, but the obvious and organized directional consumer pull is still absent. We will get there, but right now it's about investors driving down from the top and com-panies activating on their understanding of the market.

These two actions are beginning to change the face of business. We are starting to see change. When I started this, the *Economist* was not talking about disability. BBC and its Canadian counterpart, the CBC, were not talking about disability. The *Wall Street Journal* was not talking about disability. There was no disability index on the New York Stock Exchange. Now the Global Reporting Initiative, which is the accounting arm of ESG, is starting to develop a standard for disability talent. It will be watered down, it will be written in bureaucratese, it will be wholly unrelated to valuation—which suits me fine, because that means they will not be a viable competitor—but it will raise the profile of disability, and it will be codified in regulation. Regulation can be a catalyst to act—it should never be a strategy to execute.

In five years, the world will recognize that disability is the largest global emerging market. Bigger than China. Bigger than India. Something this big is hard to keep quiet. I have often said that the 1.3 billion people with disabilities are the quietest 1.3 billion people you will ever hear. That is going to change. With numbers this big, it doesn't matter what I or anybody else does. This is going to emerge. I'm just going to speed it up a bit.

CHAPTER TWENTY-FIVE
GOING PUBLIC

Ever since I created my initial basket of S&P disability out-performers, I had been having conversations with financial institutions about building an investment fund. But as I moved forward with the idea, it became clear that it was going to be difficult to do. There is a lot of regulation involved, and raising money is always tricky.

I concluded that the easiest way to get Return on Disability into the market was to set up an index and license it to somebody else to manage the financial products.

In 2013 I got a call from Johnny Wu. Johnny had been a classmate of mine at Columbia and was now running the structured products sales team for Barclays in New York. He said, "Hey Rich, I heard about the RoD product, that it performs pretty well. We're thinking about building a set of socially responsible products at Barclays. Would you like to come in and talk?" Johnny and

I had stayed connected after graduation. He had been following the progress of Return on Disability in the media and various social networks like Facebook and LinkedIn. I went in and had a conversation with Johnny and his number two, Jeff Anderson, who was also a classmate of mine at Columbia and a former colleague at Merrill, where he was in international portfolio sales and I was a portfolio trader, so we worked closely together. The three of us knew each other, we trusted each other, and we could be blunt with each other.

I explained what the index was that I had built, how I did it, what the performance was like, and what I wanted to do. Johnny said, "Well, you know, I'm not sure I want to do an actively managed fund. It's too much work, and in this regulatory environment, it would be too difficult. Would you create an index product that I could sell?"

I said, "Sure, I've already got the data, it's not that big of a leap to structure this as an index. I could create a customized product for Barclays."

Next, I had to decide how many companies to include in the index. I picked the top one hundred. It took about four months of serious negotiations with Barclays before we did the deal. We got serious with Barclays in June 2014, when we put some terms down to the agreement, drew up a contract, and went back and forth a few times; at the end of August, we signed the deal.

I can tell you that change happens one on one. You can't give a speech to a billion people and expect change to occur. People must change what they do in their daily lives, both within institutions and in their interactions with those organizations. So for every institution, you're looking at hundreds if not thousands of small changes. Multiply that by the number of institutions we have, whether those be companies, brands, or governments, and it quickly adds up to billions and billions of new actions. The Barclays deal was one of those actions.

I rang the opening bell at the NYSE to launch the RODI Fund on September 12, 2014—twelve years after the start of my career at Merrill. That was a big deal for Return on Disability. It put us on the map. Barclays launched an ETN, or exchange-traded note. That is a promise to pay at a point in time with a specified return. In this case, RODI is a ten-year obligation—the term of the note—sold in fifty-dollar slices (like shares), where Barclays will pay the holder fifty dollars per share plus the return of the index. It is a synthetic note with no leakage. With an ETF, or exchange-traded fund, which is what most people are familiar with, you hold the stock. There can be leakage regarding trading cost, regarding tracking, regarding where the actual securities that underpin the ETF are bought and sold. With an ETN, you are getting an exact return on the index. No trading cost, no tracking error.

The ETN is focused on institutional investors. I learned an awful lot going through this process. It was fantastic. I have been trading products like this for decades, but I had never created a security from just a concept. It was educational to see what was involved. Now we are working on other securities.

The next market we are looking at it is retail investing. We are building an ETF and a mutual fund because these are the popular models for individual investors. My goal is to build up investment indices country by country, then combine them into one global index. RODI is now, at the time of writing, forty-three months into live trading, and it is performing well. If it continues to perform as it has, this effort will be successful. The ultimate marker of success and the change that follows is investor returns.

At the same time as we were launching RODI, I was working to bring on new research and advisory clients. I realized that I could package the observations from the S&P 500 research into a competitive analysis of company x versus its peers. I could produce a report and sell it at a reasonable cost, one that would leverage the model, download observed best practice, and recommendations on strategy for the next three years.

In our first few years with PepsiCo, we were responsive to the needs of the team, but to project the knowledge we had built over the last five years, we needed an engagement process, one that was repeatable and scalable both for the client and for The Return on Disability Group. The first Return on Disability Report was delivered to PepsiCo in March 2013, formalizing the process we began in March 2008. We could now take that product to other clients.

I was new to sales in that my mainstream career was as a hybrid quant/trader, but, as my father told me, I had been selling since the precursor to Lime—and had become skilled at articulating the value proposition. Most of the best thinking on sales success agrees that consultative relationships and custom service lead to the best outcomes, and that is how we worked already.

What I lacked was a process. I required a clear understanding of what it took to marshal a sale from opening a new relationship to closing a deal to delighting a client. Ironically, I had already mastered the hard part: building the product and process that delights the client. Now I needed to acquire more clients to delight.

Toronto-Dominion Bank (TD) joined as our second client. My pitch was mainly this: "I have developed a model that will give you a corporate-wide strategy in disability." I structured it as a turnkey product that a company could insert into their operations. I maintained the same fundamentals but customized our recommendations. That was attractive to TD because they wanted an enterprise-wide solution and valued the independent nature of my analysis—it was not tied to an award or a charitable donation.

On a personal note, I was thrilled to see a Canadian bank acting in the disability market in more meaningful ways. As an undergraduate student at York University in the mid- to late nineties, I could not even get an interview with the Big Five Canadian banks for a teller job, much less as a risk manager or trader. Yes, it was because of my disability. And yes, it was Citibank's gain that they hired me into a risk-management role. The last fifteen years had shown progress, especially at TD. My job was to accelerate that progress. Oh, and by the way, it would be significantly easier for me to get hired out of school as a person with a disability today at a Canadian bank. We're not at the optimal point yet—one bank has ten thousand applicants with disability per year, while another has two hundred applicants—but we're moving forward.

In Canada, TD was already a leader on the disability recruiting side. They had spent decades acting to attract PWD as talent and had learned how to do it by trial and error. The next phase in TD's approach needed to focus on the customer, and I was the only guy talking about that aspect of disability with a proven model of success. For them, the customer piece was exciting. We coach our clients that the best way to start acting in disability markets is to focus on the customer, but TD had a productive recruitment and training program, which was used to show senior management a path to success. They are still a Return on Disability Group client as well as the market leader in disability in Canada.

It is often hard to sell to the best because they think they don't need your help. But the reality is that no company today is doing so well that it can't improve. Even TD still must get their enterprise-wide strategy built and executed. Part of my challenge is getting in front of as many corporate leaders as I can. We have just launched a sales campaign designed to take our coverage from seven large clients today to forty tomorrow, out of a possible five thousand in North America and Europe. The goals after that include getting to $20 million in revenue, hiring a world-class research team, breaking into Europe, and applying what we do in disability markets to women, other cultures, and LGBTQ markets. We have learned that our model and approach is applicable across markets and various segments that may do things differently.

Thus the mission of our company: translate different into value.

So the tumbleweed is gone. The crickets are gone. There is just one cricket left. We still must sell this. We are talking to some of the biggest pension funds and most loved brands in the world, and what they want to know is our methodology. They want to understand why this is different. They are so used to hearing "nice to do" when it comes to socially responsible activity that they must adjust to a new paradigm when we talk about offering real value and real returns based on actions that positively impact revenue and cost. What we do is very similar to the core of what business does every day, yet so unique in the SRI and CSR space that people don't get it at first. It's a bit surreal. But that is merely a factor of this being new. Not a lot of people understand it, and not a lot of people know they need it.

Jenn teases me by comparing me to Steve Jobs—which I take as a humbling compliment from a slightly biased wife and business partner. Jobs did many things well, but the thing he and his team did insanely well was forecasting demand. The iPod was revolutionary, but it was essentially a new delivery system for a well-understood demand—music. It was a product that no one knew they needed until they bought one. There are parallels in disability—and they go deeper than first glance. I know we have something very good. My challenge is the same as that of any entrepreneur: selling an excellent product where I know there is demand but the customer might not be able to articulate that demand. That is typical with most innovations—going in and understanding a customer's demand better than they do and coaxing it into a sale. I do less of that now than I did five years ago. Then I was like a guy selling an iPad to Walkman users: "What are you talking about?" Now it's an easier conversation because the notion of disability as a market is far more accepted than it was when I began.

Since RODI launched, I get calls from all over the world from people who are supposed to be experts on this market. I go to conferences put on by people I respect, and they will talk about disability and value, and I am grossly disappointed by the content, every time. I was at one conference a couple of months ago, put on by a group whose acumen I respect—they are one of the best economics brain trusts in the world—and their content on disability was elementary . . . I mean, I would call it vanilla, but that would be an insult to vanilla. I expected far better. That tells me that the market hasn't moved enough. I mean in the business world. The disability market has moved enormously. This space needs to find its future relevance with PWD—and that will require an investment in change that has so far failed to materialize.

When I started in this field, I was public enemy number one. People kept their distance from me because I came at this from a cold, left-brain, economic point of view. People in the space were successful at their shtick, which was dealing with fear, pity, and this notion of giving a handout. Charity. I think most people looked at me and said, "He'll go away in a couple of years. He won't survive. He'll be gone."

Now I'm standing; they're not. The ones who are left have stopped shooting arrows, have stopped trying to tear me down. It didn't bother me that they weren't playing nice—it told me that I was on the right track. When the market you are trying to change agrees with you, it means that you're not pushing hard enough. There weren't many people agreeing with me at the start of this. A lot of people still feel threatened. Small wonder, since the U.S. government spends more than half as much money on disability as they do on defense. There are many interests in keeping the status quo.

Think about that for a second. Each year, U.S. federal government payments for disability-related program spending total more than $350 billion. That's a lot of livelihoods. That's a lot of administrative work, that's a lot of small businesses, that's a lot of consulting, that's a lot of people who make a living maintaining a system that everyone agrees must drastically change. They're keeping the system maintained. They're not incentivized to change. Because they have a pretty good lifestyle. There is a lot of money that wants to keep the system exactly the way it is. That's not evil, that's not wrong, it's just how people built the system. Society has evolved, yet the methods of the past remain.

I used to joke with Jenn that I should probably get Secret Service protection. That is only half a joke. Ari Ne'eman received multiple death threats as he was being confirmed by the U.S. Senate after being appointed by President Obama to the National Council on Disability. That's a wake-up call for those of us pounding the table, demanding something we see as natural. Reality is dirty sometimes. That so many people disagree with people like Ari and me tells you how much friction there is against change. It's going to take time, it's going to take energy, it's going to take new ideas, and it's going to take deliberate actions to fulfill demand. All those things are quite complex. There's only one way to do it, and that's one gritty step at a time.

When I meet with advisory prospects, I see first-hand how much work there is to do. One of the first things they say is, "Rich, my company gave $x million to disability charities last year."

"Okay," I will answer. "What impact did that have on your business?"

"Well, it gave us PR value."

"Bullshit" is my most frequent response. I say "bullshit" in meetings now. "How much PR value did it give you?"

"Well, we figure we got about three or four million in PR."

"Oh yeah? What was your revenue last year?"

"$48 billion."

"So, explain to me how three or four million in PR is going to impact a revenue base of $48 billion. Explain to me how that PR is going to raise your revenue by 2 to 5 percent a year, which is what your goal should be in disability markets."

I say precisely that in meetings, in exactly that tone. And it usually gets an uncomfortable laugh, because they know I'm right. Astute investors get there themselves. Charities are another matter. They will call me up and say, "Hey Rich, company x gave us $5 million last year. Why aren't they on your list?"

And I'll say, "Well, they gave you $5 million last year and then they walked away from your rubber-chicken dinner. They didn't hire anyone, market to anyone, build any product for anyone. They're bullshit. You're getting money to keep your lights on, and they're trying to buy your stamp of approval."

Disability charities don't share my point of view. One of the things they are selling is "you'll get a profile in the disability world." One of the first lessons I teach my clients is that disability charities and agencies are not the market. The market isn't within the many lanes of the Washington Beltway. The market is in Ohio on the couch. The market isn't a CEO of a charity who gets paid $500,000 to push paper around and get 2 percent increases in revenue every year. He's not changing the world. He's keeping his staff paid and keeping the lights on. I've seen it. I've sat on the boards of these places. I would give an airline far more credit for simplifying their process for getting PWD from the curb into airplanes, which would cost $1 million to figure out, than to stick their logo on a charity website for $5 million. You get zero credit for the $5 million; you get lots of credit for the $1 million. Why? Because you've delighted your customers, you've caused them to give you more money, and you've likely made it easier for all your customers to travel.

CHAPTER TWENTY-SIX
THE CHARITY FALLACY

The reason why what I'm doing hasn't been done in every industry everywhere around the world is simple. Too many people look at disability, and they see a pathetic bunch of people who cannot possibly be consumers. That is what they've been told by charities that need to raise money. What if one of your neighbors started raising money to hire a tutor for your kids because they heard they weren't getting As in chemistry, and they did it without asking you?

Charities have companies believing that writing them a check is money better spent than trying to figure out how to invest that money in their ecosystems to attract customers and talent who happen to have disabilities. Think about it. Donating money to a charity is abstract, transactional, and requires no engagement. It's far easier; I'll give you that. Is it impactful on your customers, employees, or investors? Unlikely.

Donating to an autism foundation for its annual dinner, compared to actively recruiting people with autism to build long, value-added careers in your company: which one do you think will have the bigger impact on the world?

In the worst-case scenario, companies give charities money for protection. Think of big polluters that donate to environmental organizations. They do it so that they can point to the good they are doing that counters the bad. The market is smarter than that now, and consumers see right through it.

The proof that wholesale charity doesn't work—I say "wholesale" because charity does have its place—is in the numbers. A fifth of the world has a disability, yet disability charities are lucky if they can pay their bills. If they were even thinking about altering the path of a billion people, they would be thriving. If you want to look at charities that make a difference in the world, look at the Gates Foundation or the Clinton Global Initiative. These organizations are doing things like empowering entire continents to actively participate in the global economy. Now that's change. That is an aggressive and measurable goal. Disability charities aren't even in the same zip code. They need to respond to their history of failing to produce the state of the world that they promised PWD they would provide. That's the responsibility of a nonprofit that truly serves its constituents—including taxpayers.

The most convincing proof that some charities are spinning their wheels is that the only measurement they are using is dollars raised. And I get that. That's the way it's done. But if I do my job right, every corporation should be asking, "*Why* am I giving money? Can't we do something that will bring me customers or deliver some other economic benefit?" Those are the only two questions they should be asking. Those two questions will change the way that charities operate. If a charity comes to company x and the firm says, "I'm not sponsoring you next year unless you change your process," it's going to happen. No question. It will happen organically. Donors are eventually going to say, "Your approach has failed, we want something different." And they will get it.

I was invited to a disability charity gala recently. One of the highlights of the evening was a celebration of an athlete who plays sledge hockey. I thought to myself, *Okay. This guy is no doubt an outstanding sledge hockey player. But are these folks spending all this energy on sledge hockey when there are so many other things that they could be doing? Am I in the Twilight Zone here?* That gala probably raised $4 million. When I think of that, I get a little steamed. I've done *all* of this on less than $1 million. Return on Disability, Lime, everything. If I had $4 million, I could bloody well change the world! And these guys raise it in a dinner—a dinner celebrating something that just does not impact the lives of 99.95 percent of PWD. I have not checked the data, but judging by these celebratory dinners, one might quickly conclude that most PWD are world-class athletes. I am going to assert that they are not and that we may wish to highlight achievements in culture, science, and economics. You know, reflect reality.

On that same subject, I would like to make a prediction. I foresee the death of disability sports within ten years. The Paralympics and events like it are anachronistic concoctions that were created by doctors fifty years ago because they didn't know what to do with all these kids in wheelchairs and war veterans. As PWD, we are telling people that we don't want to be segregated, but every four years we're supposed to celebrate being segregated? Wrong.

Here's a thought. Wheelchair basketball. If your dream is to play in the Olympics and you are cut from the Team USA basketball squad, and you decide you want to go try out for the wheelchair basketball team, and it's a sport in the Olympics, are you allowed to try out?

Well, why the hell not? I think we should tear down all the

barriers. Put the viable disability sports into the Olympics and open them up to all athletes. You might have to add two or three days to the spectacle because there will be more events, but so be it. There should be no Paralympics. I have a disability, and I became a good sailor—an Olympic event, by the way. I bet an elite four disabled people could run a bobsled as well as any able-bodied crew.

Some of these sports are entirely viable. Not all of them. We have to stop treating them like they're all legitimate. To move forward, we need to distance ourselves from that. My solution is simple: if a sport is viable even with an adapted class, put it in the Olympics. If it's not an athletic achievement meritorious of an Olympic event, get rid of it. Because it's doing a disservice to people with disabilities everywhere, who live in the "real world." It reinforces a radioactive brand.

As a society, we value four things: education, work, family, and fun. Everything that we celebrate in disability is in the fun camp. And while I'm all for fun, to be taken seriously in this world, the first three things are far more important. I know why we are still caught in the fun paradigm: muscle memory. It's a lot easier to get an award printed out on a piece of Lucite, dress a bunch of guys up in Team Canada jackets, and stuff a room full of corporate sponsors than work out how the other pieces of the puzzle fit.

CHAPTER TWENTY-SEVEN
A BILLION BELLS

At the time of writing, the Return on Disability Index has been outperforming the S&P 500 by 2.82 percent a year over the last five years. In Canada, we put the top fifty companies for disability against the TSX Composite Index and have been consistently outperforming the benchmark by about four hundred basis points, or roughly 4 percent annually. Every investor is looking to get that kind of performance with the same risk as the market.

We update the index annually, based on assessments of each firm in our research universe. Turnover from the index happens in two ways: a) new companies that are doing things better than the bottom tier of old companies, and b) mature companies getting taken over, merging, or divesting assets. You're not going to see many mergers amongst large firms, so new entries are responsible for most of the turnover.

It took three years to develop the RoD model and five years to build the base of data. Every year, we update company data and continuously improve the model. That's easy to do as of 2018, because the market is not on fire with change. Companies are not yet competing to outdo their peers in disability. This is starting to change, and the rate of change is increasing—slowly.

Our research and advisory client base continues to grow as we convert our observations into strategy and action plans for clients. We're seeing investors getting more comfortable with a return-driven approach to socially responsible investing. In the not too distant future, we will have indices on every continent. RoD is earning demand in the U.K., South America, and Asia, and is attracting attention in Australia.

The most impressive indication of success has been from existing clients asking us to apply RoD principles to other markets—women, race/culture, and LGBTQ. One CEO I met with recently went so far as to suggest that any business can adopt our approach as a core business strategy of any company—focused on delighting the customer. As a quality guy, I take this customer feedback seriously—these are the organizations that must change to meet society's stated objectives.

I know Return on Disability is not an easy concept. It seems easy, but it's not. I still catch people that I work with closely talking about this as an HR-only endeavor. When people introduce me at speaking events, their introduction usually misses the mark. When they listen to what I have to say, they go, "Oh. I misread that one; I get it now." I understand we are working a long game. Understanding Return on Disability takes multiple conversations; it takes seeing it work in the marketplace to create real understanding.

When you're creating a new market, it takes time and a thick skin. It requires that you step on a few toes. An equivalent is nation-building. If you want to reinvent a country, you had better be ready for a prolonged process. People aren't going to be happy with what you're doing. Getting to the point of understanding and acceptance is a process that takes years and sometimes decades. I have given the same presentation of facts and methods hundreds of times. It's just what has to happen. Repetition, repetition, repetition. And then more repetition.

My ultimate vision is to have Return on Disability adopted in every primary market in the world, incentivizing corporations and governments to change their behavior to serve PWD as customers and hire PWD as employees. Recently, I've expanded my vision to include all non-traditional markets. When I say "vision," I don't mean that I am going to wave my magic wand and *poof*, success will magically appear. People think vision is magical. Vision is taking a swing. It's imagining what could be and working out the consequences of the future state that you envision. Then working your way back from that to take the actions that must happen to create that vision.

That's how you turn vision into a business or a service or a nonprofit or whatever vehicle you want to end up with: you create the process and measurable actions necessary for that vision to occur. It's all very logical, but you have to take a position. And in taking a position, you're going to be at least partly wrong. There's no way you're going to be all the way right. I can't tell what's going to happen in four years. Nobody can. But you adjust. You set a path forward based on that vision, and as conditions change, you adjust to keep moving toward it. That's what happened with writing this book. I wrote an article two years ago that Jenn particularly liked, and the light bulb went on, and she suggested I start working on a book.

I admire the Japanese approach to vision. In particular, a certain company that makes large machines and has a forty-year vision of being number one in the global housing market. When a manager looks at growth, they look at how they are going to position themselves for the next month, quarter, or year. A visioneer looks at long-term growth and positioning and sets thresholds. It's not commonly done, and I credit my father for getting me to think like that. I am playing it out like a chess game, twenty-seven moves ahead. That involves creating new language, new constructs, and new methodologies to measure activity. A lot of out-and-out creating new "stuff."

Return on Disability is the first step to achieving that forty-year vision. Not the last step. The first. I call it a forty-year vision, but it may come to pass in five years. It may take eighty. But if you don't set a stake in the ground and say, "This is where we are going," and clearly delineate the things that must happen to create that state, you are never going to get there. If it's just my team of six people doing this, it is going to take forty years, and I will be eighty by the time we're done. I trust that others will step forward to build those things that have to happen.

The key to success? It must be exciting enough to entice people to want to make it real. A forty-year vision of a company that grows at 2 percent per year is not exciting. A market that represents half the world and grows into $30 or $40 trillion in disposable income in forty years? Now you've got my attention.

My forty-year vision for disability is simple. I want to convince the institutions that we know and love, both private and public sector, to step forward and attract PWD to add value in everything that they do. My vision begins with the kind of conversation that women enjoy today. Recent research has convinced me that even efforts to serve women are far shallower than I imagined. To realize potential value, deeper connections between these markets and the organizations that seek to attract them are needed.

Equality doesn't mean parity. It's about having access to the same financial, human, or social capital that the rest of the world has. Traveling all over the continent with Lime, recruiting the best people, I quickly discovered that PWD don't constitute some monolithic block of people. These are real people living everyday lives. They have hopes, they have dreams, they have demands, just like everybody else. They will respond to change in public institutions like education, but the most powerful response will come as a result of an adjusted service mechanism within brands, companies, and governments.

To make this vision real, these institutions must believe that there is value in serving this market and attract this market as both customers and talent. To attract people, one must be attractive. Not merely inclusive. It sounds simple, but nobody is thinking that way today. In making oneself attractive, one understands demand and serves it. On a global scale, that means hundreds of thousands of institutions changing how they act in disability, and within those institutions, hundreds of millions of individuals changing how they act in disability. It's a big job.

It's a new model that breaks the old one into pieces. My father used to say, "If something is halfway broken and it's not usable, break it all the way. And force yourself to create something that's better." People aren't breaking anything yet; they are accepting a system that is less than perfect. If you are not achieving the things you need to acquire your vision, break it all the way. Build something better. If you can't do that, get the hell out of the way.

We live in an age where reinvention is a daily occurrence. We have unbelievably influential institutions that did not wield nearly as much power ten years ago. Google is a good example. There will be new institutions that influence society in five years' time that we don't know about today. So changing behavior is far from impossible, but it requires concrete action to accomplish it. My vision hinges on the ability to entice disruptors into disability, a rarity today because disruptors do not yet see the opportunity. Disruptors can do whatever the hell they want because they are exceptionally talented. My job is getting them to play in this space. The only way I know how to do that is by proving that profits are real. Serving 53 percent of the population is profitable; there is money to be made here. I know this like I have four fingers and a thumb on my left hand. Disrupters follow the money. Always have, always will. Get them on board and they will figure out how to build the infrastructure to serve these new markets.

For the business leaders considering these arguments, your competition has already started. When fragmented communities discover their economic clout and unify behind it, they wield immediate power. They reward the companies that understand their demands and adjust their offerings to delight with loyalty. They want to work for these companies. They want to spread the word. They don't need a pat on the head or empty rhetoric. They need to be wooed.

To people with disabilities and their friends and families, own your identity and demand the experiences that you want. Embrace the things that you believe make you different. Make them your biggest assets. Unleash yourself. I'm not talking about marching on global capitals, although that is one expression of demand. Emphatically share with global brands what delights you, and aggressively reward the leaders when they act. Help the laggards by assertively, calmly, and constructively telling them what they get wrong. Great organizations listen to their customers and strive to be attractive to their employees. Punish those that do not change their behavior by spending your $8 trillion and taking your valuable talent somewhere else. Not all will change, but enough will act if you demand it. Do not settle for mere inclusion. Demand delight.

I have learned that you cannot tell people how to change, you must show them how to change. The best that I can do is to paint a picture of what the future looks like and start to create it. People have to believe that change is in their best interest and figure out how to do it for themselves. Instead of acting alone, head-down, my job is to paint a picture of what the future looks like and entice others to join me in ringing the opening bell for people with disabilities around the world. One bell is a signal. Twenty bells are an alarm. One billion bells can move the world to change the future. I want to get those billion bells ringing.

ACKNOWLEDGMENTS

In writing this book, Jenn Donovan pushed me outside my comfort zone to tell my story. We tried to find that balance between a very personal journey and helping the market discover disability as a material source of economic growth. Thanks to Jenn, we got there. Thank you for being my partner in life and in business. I did promise you interesting. To my son, Maverick, thank you for pushing me to keep this book grounded in reality—a seven-year-old is a great test subject—and thanks for giving me lots of play breaks to reset my brain.

Thanks to Carl Michener for planting the seeds of this book in my head and for his work in writing this book with me. Carl was instrumental in finding and onboarding our literary agent, as well as managing the project through to proposal submission.

Herb Schaffner and Big Fish Media brought the book to life.

He was able to tell this story in a way that appeals to two very different audiences—no easy feat. Thank you, Herb.

As I was a first-time author, my literary agent, Leah Spiro at Riverside Creative Agency, was instrumental in showing me the way through the process with a strong focus on a quality product. Leah, thank you for being both a teacher and an ally.

To the team at ECW Press—you rock! You managed us through this process, on time, with a fastidious focus on quality and meeting demand. Thank you.

Finally, to the thousands of people with disabilities that I've met since 2005, thank you for sharing with me. It is amazing what one learns when one dares to ask tough questions. Keep answering, please.

At ECW Press, we want you to enjoy this book in whatever format you like, whenever you like. Leave your print book at home and take the eBook to go! Purchase the print edition and receive the eBook free. Just send an email to ebook@ecwpress.com and include:

- the book title
- the name of the store where you purchased it
- your receipt number
- your preference of file type: PDF or ePub

A real person will respond to your email with your eBook attached. And thanks for supporting an independently owned Canadian publisher with your purchase!